STREET
FIGHTERS

STREET FIGHTERS

The Last 72 Hours
of Bear Stearns,
the Toughest Firm
on Wall Street

KATE KELLY

PORTFOLIO

PORTFOLIO

Published by the Penguin Group
Penguin Group (USA) Inc., 375 Hudson Street,
New York, New York 10014, U.S.A.
Penguin Group (Canada), 90 Eglinton Avenue East, Suite 700, Toronto,
Ontario, Canada M4P 2Y3 (a division of Pearson Penguin Canada Inc.)
Penguin Books Ltd, 80 Strand, London WC2R 0RL, England
Penguin Ireland, 25 St. Stephen's Green, Dublin 2, Ireland
(a division of Penguin Books Ltd)
Penguin Books Australia Ltd, 250 Camberwell Road, Camberwell,
Victoria 3124, Australia (a division of Pearson Australia Group Pty Ltd)
Penguin Books India Pvt Ltd, 11 Community Centre,
Panchsheel Park, New Delhi–110 017, India
Penguin Group (NZ), 67 Apollo Drive, Rosedale, North Shore 0632,
New Zealand (a division of Pearson New Zealand Ltd)
Penguin Books (South Africa) (Pty) Ltd, 24 Sturdee Avenue,
Rosebank, Johannesburg 2196, South Africa

Penguin Books Ltd, Registered Offices: 80 Strand, London WC2R 0RL, England

First published in 2009 by Portfolio, a member of Penguin Group (USA) Inc.

3 5 7 9 10 8 6 4 2

LIBRARY OF CONGRESS CATALOGING IN PUBLICATION DATA
Kelly, Kate.
Street fighters : the last 72 hours of Bear Stearns,
the toughest firm on Wall Street / by Kate Kelly.
p. cm.
Includes index.
ISBN 978-1-59184-273-6
1. Bear, Stearns & Co. 2. Investment banking—United States.
3. Bank failures—United States. 4. Financial crises—United States. I. Title.
HG4930.5.K45 2009
332.660973—dc22   2009007694

Printed in the United States of America
Set in Minion   Designed by Francesca Belanger

To the 14,000 people
who worked at Bear Stearns

CAST OF CHARACTERS

At The Bear Stearns Companies
Alan Schwartz, chief executive
Sam Molinaro, chief financial officer
Bob Upton, treasurer
Tom Marano, head of mortgages
Paul Friedman, chief operating officer of the fixed-income division
Jimmy Cayne, chairman
Alan "Ace" Greenberg, director and former CEO
Vincent Tese, lead director
Richie Metrick, investment banker
Carl Glickman, director
Tim Greene, cohead of the fixed-income funding desk
Steve Meyer, cochief of the equities division
Pat Lewis, deputy treasurer
Jeff Mayer, cohead of the fixed-income division
David Kim, internal lawyer
Steve Begleiter, head of corporate strategy

At JPMorgan Chase & Co.
Jamie Dimon, chairman and CEO
Steve Black, cochief of the investment bank
Bill Winters, cochief of the investment bank
Matt Zames, head of foreign-exchange and interest-rate product
    trading
Steve Cutler, general counsel
Doug Braunstein, head of corporate finance

At the Federal Reserve

Tim Geithner, president of Federal Reserve Bank of New York

Ben Bernanke, chairman of the Federal Reserve Board

Kevin Warsh, governor of the Federal Reserve Board

At the U.S. Department of the Treasury

Hank Paulson, secretary

Bob Steel, undersecretary

Advisers to Bear Stearns

Gary Parr, deputy chairman of Lazard Ltd.

Rodge Cohen, chairman of Sullivan & Cromwell LLP

Dennis Block, senior partner, Cadwalader, Wickersham & Taft LLP

At J.C. Flowers & Co., LLC

Chris Flowers, founder

Jacob Goldfield, adviser

John Oros, managing director

Third Parties

Lloyd Blankfein, chairman and chief executive of Goldman Sachs
    Group, Inc.

Gary Cohn, copresident of Goldman Sachs Group, Inc.

Josef Ackermann, chairman of Deutsche Bank AG

John Mack, chairman and chief executive of Morgan Stanley

Warren Buffett, chief executive of Berkshire Hathaway Inc.

PREFACE

This book was born of a three-part series I wrote for the *Wall Street Journal* in May 2008 about the demise of The Bear Stearns Companies. Published two and a half months after a devastating run on the investment bank, the articles detailed the battle for survival that had been waged inside Bear during its waning months and days as its employees fought fearful lenders, hesitant trading partners, and, worst of all, clients who had lost their faith.

The series struck a chord with many *Journal* readers; after its publication, I received hundreds of e-mails and phone calls with comments—the vast majority admiring. But the most gratifying feedback came from a father of two young children who had worked in Bear's equities department. When his kids were old enough, he said, he planned to give them the *Journal* stories to read. "Then," he told me, "they'll understand what happened to Daddy's career." His words underscored the brutal impact that the Bear Stearns collapse—and the credit crisis that spurred it—has had on hundreds of thousands of workers in the U.S. economy.

For *Street Fighters*, I selected the most dramatic three days of the Bear saga and examined them hour by hour; from the evening of March 13, when Bear executives realized they were nearly out of cash, to the evening of March 16, when Bear directors approved the firm's original sale to J.P. Morgan for $2 per share. I wanted to take readers through that agonizing weekend as if they'd been inside 383 Madison Avenue themselves. I hope I've succeeded.

I am deeply indebted to the roughly one hundred people who availed themselves to me for interviews. The vast majority did so anonymously, with the understanding that their recollections would not be attributed to them by name, job description, or employer. Scenes containing direct quotes or thoughts were reconstructed through interviews with the subjects themselves or, where that wasn't possible, with close associates of those subjects who were familiar with their words and thoughts. I have attempted to corroborate those quotes, thoughts, and situations with all the relevant parties. Cases in which a speaker strongly disagreed with other sources' recollections of his or her quotes or thoughts—or in which the speaker refused to comment on the quote one way or another—have been footnoted in the text

This book would not have been possible without the help of many friends, colleagues, and advisers. I am grateful to Robert Thomson, the *Journal*'s editor in chief; Nik Deogun, deputy managing editor; and Ken Brown, money and investing editor, for granting me book leave. Thanks go also to Mike Siconolfi, Mike Williams, and Alex Martin, the troika of editors who brought the original series to life. I owe particular recognition to Mike Siconolfi, my mentor and friend, for his ongoing advice and support.

For their time, encouragement, and wisdom along the way, I thank Greg Ip, Sarah Ellison, Bruce Orwall, Seth Mnookin, and Michael Lewis. For their tireless handling of my many questions and enthusiasm for the book, I thank my editor, Adrienne Schultz, and my publisher, Adrian Zackheim; without them this would never have come together. Thanks to Bob Barnett, Tom Hentoff, and Bonnie Nathan, who gave invaluable advice, legal and otherwise, and to Scott White and Brian Rance, for their sound technical advice. Finally, my immense gratitude to Yana Collins Lehman, Felice Tebbe, Megan Hickey, and the rest of my inner circle in Park Slope.

Most important, I thank my loving husband, Kyle Pope; my parents, Pat and Joe Kelly; my stepdaughter, Laney Pope; and our boy, Bogart, for their patience and support.

Kate Kelly
February 2009

THURSDAY
March 13, 2008

5:30 P.M.

Early on the evening of Thursday, March 13, Sam Molinaro, chief financial officer of The Bear Stearns Companies, called the firm's CEO, Alan Schwartz. "We have a serious problem," Molinaro said.

Up in his forty-second-floor office, Schwartz had been hearing snippets of bad news all afternoon. Bear traders, trying to do business with rival firms, were getting pointed questions about whether they could make good on their financial obligations, and hedge funds had been yanking money out of their Bear accounts. By the time he got the call from Molinaro, Bear's cash supply appeared to be draining fast.

"This is looking pretty serious," Schwartz replied. "I'll be right down."

Schwartz took the elevator to the sixth floor, where executives were slowly congregating outside Molinaro's corner office. Though no one had sent out an e-mail, the word got around that the firm's top managers were meeting at 6:00.

Like many meetings led by Molinaro, however, the tone seemed to be one of hurry up and wait. Bear's CFO was hopelessly disorganized, and had a knack for making important people hang around outside his office while he wrapped up a phone call or had an impromptu meeting. The delays sometimes lasted for hours. Molinaro's chaotic scheduling was so widely remarked on that Paul Friedman, the sardonic chief operating officer in the fixed-income division, liked to sum it up with a joke: "What time is our six o'clock meeting?"

This time, Molinaro was tied up in his office with his former secretary, now a managing director in the firm's operations department, which handled Bear's real estate dealings around the world.

Knowing the urgency of the meeting they awaited, managers rolled their eyes as they glanced from their watches to their BlackBerrys outside Molinaro's adjoining conference room.

Finally Molinaro walked in and took a seat. Schwartz, at fifty-seven a towering, impeccably dressed former baseball star, sat near the door at the head of the table, legs crossed, silently leaning back in his chair. He had not expected this when he was named CEO barely three months earlier.

He was surrounded by a wily group of fellow executives who over the years had supported one another, challenged one another, and vied for one another's jobs and pay. Bear was a dysfunctional family, driven by greed and a complex code of internal politics. Far above the lower and middle ranks, where most of the firm's fourteen thousand employees worked, was an upper tier of some seven hundred senior managing directors, or SMDs, who made fat bonuses and enjoyed perks like a private lunch room, special expense accounts for ordering meals and flight upgrades, and unique access to key clients and public figures. Partly to justify their pay, management forced SMDs to give a small portion of their annual compensation to charitable causes, and tax returns were reviewed to make sure people complied. ("Trust but verify" was the motto governing the philanthropic program. Though many of Bear's senior managers were civic-minded, enforcement was still in order.)

But the vast majority of Bear's SMD pool was blissfully unaware of the firm's inside workings. As at most investment banks, its levers were pulled exclusively by a short list of managers who ran divisions like fixed income, equities, and prime brokerage, which handled trading and lending to Bear's most important hedge fund clients. Managers in places like risk management and operations were considered less important to the firm's core franchise and therefore largely excluded from important decisions.

Tonight's gathering, at which nearly all the power players were present, guaranteed a clash of opinions and egos. For months Bear had been struggling with a choppy stock market, plummeting home values, and an exodus of the lenders and clients that were its life-blood. The developments had created deep fissures within Bear's sharp-elbowed ruling class. The trader who ran mortgages had nearly come to blows with the cochief of equities the prior fall over whether the fixed-income department, which included the mortgage unit, deserved bonuses after such a terrible year. Bear's finance officers, who were advocating for safer ways to manage the firm's own cash, had been involved in screaming matches with their counterparts in equities who argued for the status quo. Some of Bear's top traders and executives had begged the mortgage team to divest their portfolios of its shakiest assets, to little avail. Now all the bad blood from those tumultuous months was coming to a boil.

To Schwartz's left was Richie Metrick, his longtime friend and right arm in the investment-banking business. Metrick was Schwartz's foil in nearly every respect. Short and impatient, the sexagenarian investment banker often had a stain on his shirt or a sleeve unbuttoned. Colleagues considered him something of a ball buster, a man more than willing to take them to task over disagreements. Friends praised a strong intellect that ran in his family—his son, Andrew Metrick, was a professor at the Yale business school—but many of those gathered in the conference room that evening had seen scant evidence of it since he joined Bear twenty years earlier. Mainly they knew him as Schwartz's gruff number two.

Next to Metrick was Gary Parr, the respected financial services banker from Lazard Ltd. Parr, at fifty-one, had seen his share of deals as cohead of the mergers-and-acquisitions practice at Morgan Stanley and copresident of the boutique firm Wasserstein Perella before that. More than once he had worked with insurance companies and banks on the verge of pennilessness.

The conference room they sat in had been ground zero for the internal battles of recent months, and, like much of Bear's headquarters, it was careworn from the many meetings it had hosted. The building, a forty-five-story tower of stone and glass crowned by an octagonal fixture that could be illuminated at night, was emblematic of the firm's grand visions. Designed by the noted architect David Childs, 383 Madison Avenue had been unveiled in 2001, with Bear occupying nearly every floor. It featured a square lobby with open space on all sides and a sleek, black base, just steps from Grand Central Station. A third-floor gym provided workouts and showers. The boardroom and private dining rooms were on the twelfth floor, where a private chef prepared meals. Trading floors were below, and investment banking was high above. Departments like legal, treasury, and research were on the levels in between.

Bear's new abode had already been put to good use. The prior year, the firm had hosted an array of early candidates for U.S. president, including senators Hillary Clinton and John McCain. (Barack Obama, then an Illinois senator, was invited but never committed to a date.) The private dining rooms were used to entertain clients, Wall Street analysts who watched Bear's stock, and other notables. Chairman Jimmy Cayne's office, which included a private conference room, a tricked-out motorcycle from a Chinese client whose firm Bear had taken public, and a stash of high-end imported cigars under the desk, was a particular draw.

But despite those trimmings, the inside of Bear's building was not particularly fancy. Even the sixth floor, where Molinaro, Cayne, a group of board members, and other heavy hitters resided, was essentially a warren of cubicles ringed by offices with views—mostly of the other high-rise buildings that surrounded Bear. Carl Glickman, one of Bear's longest-serving directors, had furnished his own office, spending thousands of dollars on ornate furniture, and Molinaro had a couple of nice chairs and a couch. But many executives had little other than family snapshots to look at, and the tables and chairs that Bear provided were not extravagant.

On either end of a scratched-up wood conference table, the walls in Molinaro's conference room featured symbols of a more euphoric time. One displayed a lithograph of the cover of the *Wall Street Journal* the day after the Dow Jones Industrial Average had closed at 10,000 in March 1999. IF THIS IS A BUBBLE, IT SURE IS HARD TO POP, read the headline, which was covered by a transparent bubble magnifying the zeroes in the index's record level. On the opposite wall was a framed cover of *Barron's* from 2004, when the publication had run an admiring cover story on Bear. Under the teaser "Throughout the market slide, Bear Stearns had outperformed its brethren" was a cartoonlike drawing of a brown bear dipping its paw into a honey pot as saliva dripped from its chops. The story inside called the firm "the Rodney Dangerfield" of the brokerage industry, with share-price growth that was finally generating the respect Bear had long deserved. Back then, the stock was trading at $84 a share.

Now it was at $57—a breathtaking drop from $172, where it had topped out in January 2007 during the froth of the housing boom. Record issuances of new mortgages and skyrocketing home prices throughout the United States were now collapsing under their own weight. Loans issued to "subprime" borrowers whose incomes couldn't support the expense of high-interest mortgages had, in many cases, gone into default. The defaults had prompted a wave of bank foreclosures on subprime borrower homes, forcing people to move out and harming the safety and value of other homes in surrounding neighborhoods. Fast-growing areas of states like Nevada, California, Arizona, and Florida had been especially hard hit.

In reaction to the disastrous lending practices of the housing boom, banks were providing credit to only the wealthiest, most stable consumers, leaving many potential home buyers unable to make purchases. Many of the country's most active mortgage providers, including OwnIt Mortgage Solutions and New Century Financial Corp., had gone into bankruptcy, saddled with the unwieldy costs of mortgages to subprime borrowers that had ceased to be paid down. Increasingly now, the third parties that held bonds connected to subprime loans, once those loans were "securitized" or bundled into new investments, were taking huge losses on those bonds. In a catch-22 effect, the mortgage lenders that still had money to lend were becoming leery of issuing new loans, since their ability to lay off the risk of those loans to other investors was diminishing, and the market overall was slowing to a crawl. As an issuer of new mortgages as well as a trader and holder of mortgage-backed securities, Bear was being hurt by the convulsions in the housing sector—and that was before the events of the last few days.

The mood around the table was lousy. Bear's old hands had seen more than a few competitors come and go over the years, and now their firm was uncomfortably close to becoming a Wall Street casualty. Fixed-income chief operating officer Friedman and others, who had been anxious about the firm's financing since at least last summer, were deeply frustrated. Their suggestions that the firm should sell itself or raise capital had gone largely unheeded, now with disastrous results. Schwartz, Molinaro, and some others were more shocked. They had been working their tails off for months, courting clients and shareholders and trying desperately to return Bear to profitability after its recent November quarter loss. In recent days, they'd labored to counteract the negative rumors in the market, with no success. Now, suddenly, their prized firm was on the brink of oblivion.

Dispensing with the introductions, Molinaro, who had taken a seat on the long side of the conference table not far from Schwartz, began running through a laundry list of questions. "What collateral do we have that we could repo?" he asked the group.

He was referring to repurchase agreements, otherwise known as "repo loans." Repo loans were short-term, often overnight, funding pacts, usually struck between two Wall Street firms or one firm and one investor, like a hedge fund. As the borrower, Bear would offer its counterparty—the other bank in the transaction—a bundle of securities in exchange for immediate cash. Bear could then use the cash to help fund its operations for some brief period of time, often the next twenty-four hours. Afterward, the counterparty could then return the securities to Bear, which would repay the counterparty the cash.

Much of Wall Street relied on repo loans to help finance its day-to-day operations, but Bear was more dependent on these short-term loans than its competitors were. With a leverage, or debt-to-cash ratio, of 30 to 1—meaning that for every $1 it actually held in cash, Bear had borrowed $30 from other parties—the firm had one of the heaviest debt loads of any firm on the Street. That made it more vulnerable than other firms when repo lenders faced a crisis of confidence.

To streamline the daily lending process, Bear operated financing desks in the fixed-income and equities units staffed by people whose job it was to "roll," or renew, expiring loan agreements on a nightly, weekly, or monthly basis. Eyes turned now to Tim Greene, one of the two heads of Bear's fixed-income financing desk. Greene, a West Point graduate with a soldier's sense of loyalty, had been working at Bear for twenty-four years, rising through the ranks to help run the bond unit's repo desk, which handled about $160 billion of funding at any given point—about half of Bear's entire balance sheet. He had met his wife, Maryann, on that desk, and he loved the job.

Greene was used to operating under pressure. From the time he arrived at work from suburban Connecticut at 7:00 A.M. to the time he finalized the day's funding agreements around 2:00 P.M., every day was a scramble to renew the firm's loans and keep the cash coming. Ironically, just as the stress was amping up, Greene had tried to reverse years of unhealthy eating habits with a 1,100 calorie-per-day diet and had already lost thirty pounds.

Up to now, borrowing $10 billion or $20 billion in a day generally wasn't a problem. But Friday was likely to be no average day, and the firm needed $14 billion in new money to fund its operations. On top of that, Bear had to replace, or roll, more than $10 billion.

Greene, who was facing Molinaro on the opposite side of the

room, tried to sound optimistic. His relationships with lenders ran deep, and he didn't think they'd abandon Bear overnight. "I'm confident I can do it," he told the group.

"How?" asked Molinaro.

"I can do it without anybody knowing, on the screen," Greene told him, referring to a popular computer-driven lending system in which participants could trade anonymously, without revealing their identity to the other party in the transaction.

Next to him, Greene's boss, the fifty-two-year-old Friedman, doubted it. Ever since the prior August, when two internal hedge funds had failed—giving the lie to Bear's long-vaunted prowess in careful risk management—Friedman had felt like the sky was falling. He joked to associates that he spent his days on Bear's seventh-floor mortgage-backed-securities trading hub either hiding under his desk or puking into a trash can. He hated that the funds' embarrassing failure had thrust his insular company into the spotlight.

Now Friedman told the group he thought there was no way that at least half of the next day's repo loans were going to roll in order to help fund Friday's operations. Like any trading firm, Bear spent the day buying and selling securities for itself and for clients, processes that required bundles of cash at the ready. More days than not, the firm was profitable and not losing money, but it had to be prepared to refund loans or provide additional collateral when asked. Now, with rumors sweeping Wall Street about Bear's cash drain, Friedman worried that Bear's usual lenders might be too spooked to lend as they normally would, for fear that the firm would never pay them back.

He suggested that Greene might try raising the $14 billion or so the firm had in bonds backed by Fannie Mae and Freddie Mac, government-sponsored housing agencies that were considered safer than loans packaged by other players. Those were the bonds tradable "on the screen," where no one would know it was Bear making the transactions.

Molinaro turned to his treasurer, Bob Upton, who sat across from him next to Friedman. "Where are we with cash?" he asked.

Upton studied the legal pad in front of him, on which he had jotted down his best estimates of the credits and debits in Bear's various accounts.

He felt beaten down. An unsmiling father of two, Upton had spent years toiling as an analyst of securities firms and international banks for Fidelity Investments, hoping to someday actually manage the cash at a big Wall Street firm. Since April 2006, when he had been named treasurer of Bear, the workload had been brutal. During a three-year period his dark brown hair turned almost totally white. Though he was trim, didn't drink, and watched his diet carefully, Upton now looked far older than his forty-seven years.

Like Greene, Friedman, and others, Upton and his team had suffered fallout from the hedge fund failures, as funding the firm became more difficult. For much of the past year, Upton had been arriving at work from his suburban home at 5:00 A.M., and not leaving until as late as 10:00 P.M. Many nights he got as little as four hours of sleep. I'm fucking killing myself, he often thought. Yet he, too, adored the place.

The firm's troubles had been building throughout the week. On Monday, a batch of home loans it had packaged and sold were found to be exceedingly high risk by a major rating agency, which meant that conservative investors would have to sell any of the bonds they held that were backed by those loans. Based on the headlines, some market watchers mistook the finding as a downgrade of Bear as a whole, seeing it as an indication that the company was very likely to default on its debt. Its shares tumbled. Bear was now trading at about $65 on the New York Stock Exchange.

Overnight, some of Bear's lenders—the dozens of American and overseas banks that extended it billions of dollars a day to conduct business—began tightening the reins. The Dutch bank ING refused to refresh some of Bear's credit, and others soon followed suit. Right away, Bear's major clients heard the message: The firm was no longer safe. Hedge funds like Renaissance Technologies Corp., the enormous trading firm that had long been a top client, began reducing their balance levels immediately, worrying that if Bear went down, their money would be stuck on a sinking ship. Bear shares fell further, even amid public denials by Molinaro and others that any real trouble was afoot.

Monday, Three Days Earlier

Alan Schwartz had spent the weekend in Palm Beach. He had flown there initially to attend a board dinner for one of his longtime clients, the wireless telephone company Verizon Communications, and planned to stay on for an investment conference. Things at Bear had seemed relatively calm before he'd left, and Molinaro had assured Schwartz during their frequent phone calls that business was in order.

All that changed with the ratings news on Monday. Unfortunately, the sensational headlines had driven the markets into a tizzy—prompting a precipitous dive in Bear's stock. It was a disappointing starting note for Bear's annual gathering of media investors, analysts, and executives, one of the firm's signature events.

That afternoon Schwartz met with Walt Disney chief Bob Iger, whom he was interviewing the next day at one of the conference's keynote meetings, but their prep session was interrupted frequently by calls for Schwartz from New York, where company officials were wondering how to address the market furor. After the markets closed at 4:00, Schwartz issued a statement denying that Bear faced liquidity problems. But the reaction was tepid.

Iger was no stranger to corporate calamity. Four years earlier, when he was still company president, Disney had been faced with a hostile takeover threat from the Philadelphia cable concern Comcast, resulting in a shareholder battle over the future of the entertainment company. Schwartz, as one of Disney's long-term bankers, had helped the company fight off the Comcast bid, employing his typically cool-headed diplomacy. Now, after years of advising companies under threat, Schwartz had suddenly found himself uncomfortably in the limelight.

Over dinner that night at the clubby Flagler steakhouse, across the street from the resort where the conference was being held, Iger offered his friend a word of advice: "You can't let 'em see you sweat." Whatever you do, he added, let the public and your investors know that you have the situation under control.

Tuesday

Schwartz felt he had an ace in the hole: the coming quarter's earnings results, to be announced the following week. Unbeknownst to the public and employees, the rough numbers indicated that Bear had made a profit of more than $1 per share. If only they could get to that news release, Schwartz thought, the market's anxieties would surely be calmed.

He was toying with the idea of moving the earnings announcement up and hoping to somehow hint to the marketplace that Bear was in good shape. But he would have to act soon; the share price was still low, closing at $63 on Tuesday.

Wednesday

Wednesday morning Schwartz conceded to an interview on the business-news channel CNBC to deny the rumors that Bear was failing. During the interview, he tried to sound a reassuring tone. "The markets have certainly gotten worse, but our liquidity position has not changed at all," he said. "Our balance sheet has not weakened." But suddenly the interview was interrupted by other, more pressing, news: New York Governor Eliot Spitzer, who had been linked to an illegal prostitution ring, was expected to resign from his job immi- nently. Schwartz's expression remained calm, but his mind was rac- ing. Shit, he thought. This interview is going to end and I'm not going to get any facts out.

After a few moments, the broadcast returned to him, giving an- chor David Faber a chance to quiz Schwartz about an incident in which Goldman had allegedly refused to do a trade with Bear. Schwartz seemed taken aback. "I'm not aware of that," he said. "We have direct dealings" with all the major rival firms, he added, "and we have active markets going with each one." Viewers, however, found his explanation unconvincing.*

Later that day, Schwartz flew back to New York. Bear was by then facing $2 billion in cash demands from trading partners, only $800 million of which the firm thought it actually owed. "Send it out," Schwartz told Molinaro. He didn't want anyone thinking the firm was strapped for cash. Bear shares closed that day at just under $62.*

But more requests followed, and hedge funds were by now racing for the exits, taking billions of dollars with them. Per Schwartz's instructions, trading disputes across the board were being settled in the other party's favor, and practically no money was coming in to replenish what Bear paid out. That night, Schwartz held a series of

---

*Goldman had, in fact, declined to enter a transaction with Bear late on Tues- day, March 11, and word of the incident apparently found its way to Faber. However, Goldman's decision, which had been put through the standard vetting process, was reversed the following morning, and the trade went through. After the CNBC broadcast, much was made of the matter, which some regarded as a wholesale effort on Goldman's part to freeze out Bear Stearns, exacerbating its troubles. Goldman adamantly denied those charges. "We went out of our way to be supportive of Bear Stearns," a spokesman said.

meetings with Molinaro, Upton, Steve Begleiter, the firm's head of corporate strategy, and a handful of traders. Parr, who had been attending a performance of *Macbeth* in Brooklyn, was called away from the theater during intermission.

The group pored over Bear's options for raising quick dollars. Nothing seemed workable, so they turned to a list of other companies that might be interested in an investment or a purchase of Bear. At the top of the list were J.P. Morgan, where Bear housed its own cash accounts, and the buyout firm J.C. Flowers & Co. No one thought a merger would be needed imminently, but they were preparing for the worst.

Earlier on Thursday

Thursday morning brought another big blow: an article in the *Wall Street Journal* citing Bear's trading problems. Yet the day's early hours were surprisingly quiet. The hedge fund exodus seemed to have ebbed for the moment, and trades with other firms were getting done. Traders and executives, who had been bracing for another brutal day, were breathing a sigh of relief.

Word of Bear's problems, however, was ringing alarm bells in Washington. Bob Steel, the undersecretary of the U.S. Treasury, had a troubling discussion that morning with Rodgin "Rodge" Cohen, a prominent securities lawyer who had done work for both Goldman and Bear. Shortly before a breakfast the two were scheduled to attend in the Treasury's second-floor dining room, Cohen had warned Steel that Bear faced major cash-flow problems, and that they were trying to figure out what to do. Less than an hour later, Steel was hurrying down a corridor toward his 10:00 meeting when his cell phone rang. It was his secretary, who had Schwartz on the line. The call was urgent.

"Hi, Bob," said Schwartz. "We're having some potential liquidity problems. I'm hopeful we can work through all this but I wanted to alert you."

Steel hung up and went to notify his boss, Treasury Secretary Hank Paulson, just down the hall. He walked Paulson through the talks with both Cohen and Schwartz. Bear expected to have a better handle on things by 2:00 or 3:00 that afternoon, Steel said, and they'd get an update then.

Noon Thursday

Minutes before noon, Bear managers gathered in the twelfth-floor boardroom for a scheduled meeting of the Presidential Advisory Committee, a group of forty or so top managers who advised Bear's senior brass on business matters and strategy. The day's presentations included a talk by the trader who handled Bear's commercial mortgage-backed securities. But in order to address "the environment," as the e-mailed update had put it, Schwartz was added to the speaking roster at the last minute.

No one paid much attention to the presentations until it was Schwartz's turn to talk. Despite the looming bank run, the CEO appeared uncannily relaxed. Leaning back in his chair, he dismissed the chatter around Bear's cash position, reasoning that companies like General Motors had faced similar rumor-mongering in the past that had turned out to be nothing but "noise." Bear would come out all right, he told the group, and the key was to stay focused on the day-to-day business.

But in the middle of his speech, Schwartz was interrupted by an angry Mike Minikes, the executive who ran the firm's prime-brokerage business, where hedge funds kept their money for trading. "Do you have any idea what is going on?" asked the executive. "Our cash is flying out the door. Our clients are leaving us."

Alarmed attendees waited for an answer from Schwartz, but he seemed to brush off the question. A few minutes later, with the energy drained from the room, the meeting simply broke up. While the prime-brokerage and equities-financing managers scrambled back to their posts to deal with the client refunds, others were unsure quite what to do.

An hour or two later, Molinaro, Upton, Pat Lewis, the number two man in Treasury, and other internal finance managers had gone forward with a planned meeting with the Bank of New York Mellon, one of Bear's lenders. BONY was eager to expand its lending to Bear, executives explained, but wanted to do so in a secured fashion, with assets backing up the loans. Fat chance, Upton thought to himself. Given that Bear's array of mortgage-backed bonds were declining in value and that every other creditor was making the same demands, they had few high-quality assets lying around to offer.

A bit later, Molinaro signaled Upton to come into his office.

"Bob, we're tapioca," Molinaro said.

"You gotta be fucking kidding me," Upton said. He was appalled. One minute they were discussing new funding partners, and the next the firm was out of business? It was too much to believe for one afternoon.

But Molinaro was serious. Before the BONY meeting, he explained, he had received a call from David Solomon, the Bear alum who was cochief of Goldman's investment bank. Solomon had heard the negative rumors and was witnessing, firsthand, the mass exodus from its prime brokerage, as panicked hedge fund clients contacted Goldman to see about moving their balances there.

The reason for his call, Solomon had said, was to offer Goldman's help. He emphasized that his gesture was coming from "the top of the firm," but that he had been asked to make the call because of his personal relationship to Bear.

Then he got to the point: Would Molinaro be interested in having a team from Goldman come to Madison Avenue to look over its books? Maybe to make an overnight asset purchase to help Bear raise some quick cash?

The offer left Molinaro feeling uneasy. "When Goldman calls and offers their assistance, it's usually a moneymaking opportunity for them," he told Upton. Bear wasn't dead yet, but it felt like the firm's competitors were already picking over its carcass.

Right after the BONY meeting, Molinaro had also gotten a briefing from Friedman on the state of affairs in the fixed-income repo market. Although it had been a relatively quiet day, some lenders were indicating that they wouldn't refresh Bear's funding Friday morning. It felt like everybody was turning the screws, Molinaro told Upton. Bear really might be a goner.

Upton walked down the hall to his office and took a cigar out of his desk drawer. Then he headed toward the elevator.

There are thousands of people just going about their jobs here, he thought, and they have no fucking idea that we're on the verge of collapse.

He stepped out of Bear's building, walked to the corner of Forty-seventh Street and Vanderbilt Avenue, and headed toward the breezeway carved out of the J.P. Morgan building across the street. He lit up and took a puff, staring into space. Six, seven years of working my ass off, and now the whole thing has blown up on me, he thought. He was in a state of shock.

After a few minutes, he went back to his office, closed the door, and cried. He called his wife to tell her he had no idea when he'd be home. There was little she could say to make him feel better, but it had been good to hear her voice.

7:00 P.M. Back in the Conference Room

Now Upton shared his estimates with the group. Bear had started the day with about $12 billion, he explained—north of $8 billion as of

Wednesday night, to which Bear had added another $3.5 billion or so that morning after it paid itself back money it had extended to prime-brokerage clients wanting to take their money out. But Thursday had brought an onslaught of new client demands for their cash back, as well as demands for collateral from numerous funding counterparties, leaving the firm with only about $5 billion. On top of all that, Bear that day had incurred a debt to Citigroup of about $2.4 billion—leaving Bear with less than $3 billion in total to work with.

Molinaro was now sitting bolt upright. "Okay," he sighed. "Where are we in terms of cash we can raise? What collateral can we pledge?"

Upton had brought a list of securities he thought might be salable, and he began ticking off ideas. "What about selling the Taiwan index arbitrage book?" he suggested. Heads shook. What about shrinking the U.S. rebate arbitrage book? No takers. What about some of the corporate bonds the fixed-income department still had on hand? Surely those could be liquid, or easily sold, he thought.

From the far end of the table, Tom Marano, the firm's head of mortgage trading, had been glowering. "It's T plus three," Marano said, referring to the three-day period that always elapsed between the sale of a bond and its "settlement," or the moment when the seller actually received the cash. "What good does that do us?" Bear needed cash immediately, not in three days.

Throughout the week, Marano had also heard the rumors circling the Street about predatory trading partners, like Goldman and Citadel Investment Group, gunning for Bear. He and his colleagues had also heard chatter that Deutsche Bank was shorting Bear—or betting that the firm's shares would decline in value—because traders there thought the firm might run out of money. Counteracting these bad vibes was impossible. Marano could only imagine what the big brains at the top of his firm would come up with next. He liked Molinaro, but was starting to have major doubts about Schwartz's ability to navigate such a rapidly unfolding disaster.

Upton glanced up at Pat Lewis. "What do we have in the international world?" he asked.

Standing with his back to the window, Lewis stiffened. A no-nonsense Midwesterner, he had had about enough of the shenanigans at Bear, where convincing ornery traders and disinterested executives to try new forms of more secure funding was well nigh impossible. He and Upton had been struggling to win financing from banks in Europe and Asia, markets that were notoriously difficult to crack. More conservative-minded with American firms, many had been leery about doing business with Bear initially. But after a persistent effort, Upton and Lewis had made some inroads into those markets—that was, until the two hedge funds had blown up the prior summer, humiliating Bear, costing investors $1.6 billion, and tarnishing its reputation as a creditworthy borrower.

"I'm going to go with nothing," Lewis finally said. He couldn't think of a single asset that could quickly be exchanged for cash in the international financing world.

Schwartz, who had been relatively silent through the meeting, uncrossed his legs and now sat with his hands clasped against his forehead, looking pained. Upton's secretary popped her head in to remind him that he was expected on a 7:30 P.M. call with regulators at the SEC.

Molinaro had his fingers pressed against the side of his face. This was the worst day of his twenty-two-year career, without a doubt. We're cooked, he thought. Not only will Bear have to be sold to J.P. Morgan or some other deep-pocketed bank, but we may not even be able to open the doors tomorrow.

"Guys, I don't know what our options are here," Molinaro finally said. "I think we're about out of options."

A shudder swept through the room. Schwartz abruptly rose to his feet and walked out. An equities division manager who had been standing near him wondered if the CEO was going to the men's room to vomit. He was considering doing that himself.

THURSDAY EVENING
March 13, 2008

Bear had never been long on pedigrees, but had shown a unique eye for opportunity. Lean, scrappy, and hungry for profits, the firm had an underdog's spirit, and relished the chance to knock more well-heeled Wall Street firms down a peg or two.

Its executives had never hewed to tradition in trading or investment banking; their moves were often the exact opposite of what rivals were doing. During the crash of 1929 and the Depression that followed, Bear grew staff rather than trim it. Its founding traders made their names by entering new businesses that were either untested or disrespected by the Wall Street establishment. Even its charitable requirements for SMDs, which were codified in the late 1960s, were admired, but seldom emulated, by Bear's competitors.

Bear cared little for appearances. During the 1990s, it proudly hired castoffs from competing firms who had been fired after political battles or regulatory skirmishes. A trader's outside reputation, Bear recruiters felt, had little bearing on his or her talent with a telephone, a computer terminal, and a pile of cash. In 1998, when the hedge fund Long-Term Capital Management nearly collapsed, Bear refused to participate in a bailout effort that included every other Wall Street firm. Ten years later, employees wondered if the lenders and competitors who pushed Bear to the brink were exacting revenge for the firm's selfish behavior at that time.

Bear's executives could be curt. Schwartz had an investment banker's polish, but he was a rare exception. Bear's bond traders, long the rock stars of the firm, were brusque, arrogant, and uninterested in anyone who disagreed with their positions. Their leader, the former mortgage-backed securities trader Warren Spector, set the tone. A bookish, quick thinker, the bespectacled, dark-haired executive ran his division with an iron fist, forcing even the firm's CEO to defer to his judgment. Steve Meyer, the former trader who was co-chief of the equities division, was similarly controlling. His hot temper often flared up at meetings, where he'd shout and even stand menacingly to make his point. But as a former trader of both bonds and stocks whose department had performed well over the years, he was respected and feared.

Women rarely flourished in Bear's testosterone-driven culture, where outdated behavior toward the gentler sex sometimes surfaced. In the early 1990s, the firm's executives had hired a group of scantily clad models to escort visitors from the lobby up to meetings; within the firm, they were dubbed the "geisha girls." Jimmy Cayne, the firm's CEO until Schwartz took over, liked to put out his cigars in an ashtray he'd gotten from the Women's Financial Club of New York. When a female visitor joined him for lunch, he was heard complimenting the view from behind her.

Still, Bear's tough-nosed approach to business had given the firm long legs through some very difficult times. Founded in 1923, Bear had survived the Great Depression, the Second World War, the recession in the 1970s, the crash of 1987, and the bursting of the technology bubble. Bear's risk-management models used computers to test the trades it made against market conditions from a number of those turbulent periods—and they always appeared to be safe, even under adverse conditions. Only a once-in-a-century meltdown could cause the system to collapse.

Bear had started as a small stock-trading house with less than $1 million in capital and just seven employees. They worked hard and stuck to their business. By 1933, Bear had not only survived the market crash without making layoffs, it had grown enough to purchase a small competitor in Chicago and open a branch office there. The company's ranks soon swelled to seventy-five as it entered the booming bond business.

In the late 1930s, Salim "Cy" Lewis, a powerful bond trader, took over the firm. An argumentative, six-foot-four former football player who had worked at Salomon Brothers before Bear, Lewis's rough-and-tumble persona set the stage for generations of executives to come. Lewis focused on distressed quasi-public investments like railroads and utilities, making a fortune when business began picking up. Then, in the 1950s, he pioneered the practice of making "block" trades, or buying and selling multiple shares of stock in a single transaction.

He was a strong believer in the "buy and hold" strategy, refusing to sell even losing positions. As the years wore on, this created friction with a young protégé, Alan "Ace" Greenberg. The son of a clothier from Oklahoma City, Greenberg had been hired as a clerk at Bear in 1949 and had grown into his job as a successful stock trader. He embraced a simple ethos, handed down to him by his dad: never hang on to losing inventory, because as little as it's worth today, it'll be worth less tomorrow. Greenberg argued this point with his boss repeatedly, eventually distinguishing himself as a savvy risk manager. In 1978, Lewis collapsed of a massive stroke at his own retirement party at New York City's Harmonie Club. Bear had just presented him with a watch to recognize his four decades of service. He died, leaving the reins to Greenberg, then fifty-one.

Greenberg ran the firm until 1993, when Jimmy Cayne took his spot as CEO. For most of their tenures, Bear's business bloomed. In 1985, the firm undertook a successful IPO on the New York Stock Exchange, and its shares rose phenomenally in the years that followed. Even after selling shares to the public, a move that brought outside shareholders into the mix, Bear maintained its cloistered partnership culture, fueling the internal competition that had helped it to succeed. A wildly lucrative foray into the world of mortgage-backed securities, spurred largely by Spector's arrival in the 1980s, had grown Bear's bottom line. And its prime-brokerage unit, one of the first on Wall Street, distinguished it as a servicer of hedge funds and other big traders.

Overseas and in areas like asset management, where other financial firms had begun to make significant inroads, Bear remained relatively weak. Its investment-banking unit, despite Schwartz's hard work, was a small player next to Goldman and Morgan Stanley. But during the housing boom of the mid-2000s, those things mattered little. Bear was on top, reporting huge profits, an ebullient share price, and enviable paydays for its senior people. Of the five major investment banks, it was like the little shop that could.

7:45 P.M.

Down the hall in his own office, Bob Upton dialed the speakerphone box. Matt Eichner, a senior staffer in the SEC's division of trading and markets, picked up.

"We need to give you an update on where we are," said Upton, as Lewis and Mike Alix, Bear's professorial chief risk officer, looked on. "It was not a very good day."

Eichner was used to hearing from the Bear executives. Since the prior summer, when Bear had first faced questions about its cash flow, the SEC had been monitoring Bear more closely. Regulators had set a 5:00 phone call with Upton and his team that was held daily or weekly, depending on the market environment. During the call, Upton would walk Eichner through the firm's end-of-day cash positions, explaining how much money went out and how much was brought in through the course of business.

During February and March, Bear had also been e-mailing the SEC once a day to alert it to any major changes in its cash holdings. The prior Monday, Eichner had grown somewhat alarmed by the increasing noise surrounding the firm, as rumors of prime brokerage client outflows and canceled trades multiplied. He e-mailed Upton to say that while he knew the treasurer was awfully busy, he wanted to spend some more time reviewing the numbers.

The SEC had been in touch with Bear already that day, but between their last call at 4:00 and now, things had taken a dramatic turn for the worse. Now Alix tried to paint a picture for the regulators. "Fixed income repo seems to be going away," he announced. In other words, Bear was getting early indications from creditors who lent money to its bond unit that they weren't going to come through with replenished loan money in the morning. "I don't know what the dollar amount is," Alix added.

Then he described the prime-brokerage exodus. "A lot of client money is going out the door."

Upton spoke of Friday, by now just a few hours away. If things were to miraculously stabilize, Upton said, perhaps Bear could muddle through the business day. He and his team were now cobbling together a list of assets that could be sold, he said, in hopes of raising enough cash to make it to the weekend.

Eichner said the Commission might be able to eliminate the forty-eight-hour lockup on Bear's so-called 15c3-3 money, which would allow it to receive cash it was expecting in two days on an expedited basis.

Like other Wall Street firms, Bear held cash, stocks, and bonds that belonged to its hedge fund and other clients. To protect client assets, those funds were carefully monitored, and kept in a cordoned-off account that was overseen by the SEC. They were known as 15c3-3 funds, after the SEC rule that governed them.

The amount of money Bear held on behalf of clients varied day to day, but to save time and effort, the total 15c3-3 sum was calculated only once a week. If Bear had received additional cash or securities from clients in a given week, it would add to the total, and if it had lost cash or securities, it would deplete the total. But there was a two-day holding period applied to moving money in or out of the accounts, so Bear would sometimes have to front its clients cash from its own stash, then wait forty-eight hours for the SEC to issue a refund.

Waiving the waiting period would help, the Bear team agreed.

But little could be decided until the firm had a better handle on its options for raising cash. The two groups agreed to keep each other posted, then hung up.

A moment later, Molinaro stopped in. "Did you make it clear to them the position that we're in?" he asked.

"I think they get it," said Alix, a little uncertainly.

"Call them back," said Molinaro.

Alix walked back to his office and called Eichner, who quickly got his superiors on the line as well. "I just want to make sure you understand, if you didn't perceive it before, that this is serious," Alix told the group. "We have serious doubts about our ability to operate normally tomorrow."

The regulators said they understood. The Federal Reserve and the U.S. Treasury would need to be informed, they added. Bear was in touch with Tim Geithner, Alix assured the regulators, and would be kept in the loop. It was looking increasingly possible that Bear would file for bankruptcy protection the next day.

After the big meeting broke up, Gary Parr huddled with Schwartz and Metrick to sort out their next moves. Time was of the essence, so they agreed he should contact Bear's top potential acquirers right away. Finding an empty office on a quiet stretch of the sixth floor, Parr walked in, closed the door, and picked up the phone.

Parr had advised banks, money managers, and insurers through numerous crises in the past. But even for someone of his experience, it had been a shocking day. Having worked late on Madison Avenue the prior evening, Parr had barely reached his Lazard offices Thursday morning before he was summoned back to Bear for another urgent strategy session. He, Schwartz, and others had monitored the firm's situation throughout the day, waiting to see where Bear's cash holdings would balance out. Compared to the day they had had on Thursday, Wednesday's brainstorming session seemed like a casual conversation.

In fact, Parr hadn't even thought to cancel plans he had that night to see *South Pacific* with a Lazard colleague. "Can't go," he BlackBerried the man now. "I'm working." Even with close associates, his MO was to be exceedingly vague when a client problem was live.

Schwartz and Parr had agreed that his first call would be to Jamie Dimon, J.P. Morgan's CEO. As Bear's "custodian," or the bank that ultimately transferred cash in and out of Bear's accounts when trades and loans were made, the large bank was well familiar with Bear and its positions, Schwartz and Parr reasoned. J.P. Morgan's enormous balance sheet gave it plenty of cash with which to make acquisitions, and with no prime-brokerage business of its own, the bank might find Bear's hedge fund servicing and lending unit very attractive. Best of all, Dimon, a shrewd and sharp-tongued executive, had done dozens of deals in his career and was known for his ability to move fast.

Parr was well positioned to make the phone call. He had advised Dimon on the sale of Bank One, the Chicago-based firm he ran in the early 2000s, to J.P. Morgan for $58 billion in 2004. For Dimon, it had been a career-altering move that led to his current role.

Dimon's office at 270 Park Avenue was just across the street from Bear. But when his cell phone rang, he was tucking into a celebratory dinner at a nearby Greek restaurant with his wife, parents, and one of his three daughters. It was his fifty-second birthday.

"Jamie," Parr began, "I'm sorry to bother you. But I wouldn't call if it wasn't important."

Dimon wasn't thrilled. Even when it wasn't a special occasion, he hated being interrupted on his cell phone, which was reserved largely for his kids' use. This, he figured, must be a real emergency.

"I'm calling about Bear Stearns," Parr said. "We have a real issue here and we need to be talking to you and your team. They're in desperate shape. They need a lot of money." He asked if there was any chance Dimon could make Bear a big loan that night.

Dimon's mind whirled. He couldn't fathom making a purchase

of Bear's size in just twelve hours. Still, there could be some possibilities there. He asked if Bear had been in touch with Hank Paulson or Ben Bernanke, the Fed chairman.

Parr said yes. Bear executives had been in touch with those parties all day, he said, and would continue to post them that evening as things progressed. He pressed Dimon. Though it would be tough to do an overnight deal, was he willing to explore some options? Would Dimon take a direct call from Alan Schwartz?

"I'd be happy to talk to Alan, and I can get a team on it right away," Dimon replied. By now he had walked out of the restaurant and onto East Forty-eighth Street, where he could speak more privately. He hung up and began dialing his deputies.

Geithner wasn't surprised to hear that night from Bear. Like Bob Steel, he'd received an early morning call from Schwartz, who had warned him that a cash crisis might be looming.

Geithner had spent much of Thursday talking to his staff and other regulators about the issues that faced Bear, trying to gauge how swiftly they might slide downhill. Unlike the SEC, however, he had taken cold comfort in knowing that Bear had opened that morning with close to $10 billion. What mattered, he felt, wasn't the hard cash the firm kept on hand, but how long that cash could last under such punitive market conditions. Not long, had been his guess.

Geithner had spoken to Schwartz earlier in the evening and knew he was contacting J.P. Morgan for a loan. Until he got an update, however, all the Fed official could do was wait. He was eating dinner with his wife and children at their suburban home when Schwartz called with terrible news.

"We're down to three or four billion and we feel like we've got no option but to file," Schwartz said, in a pointed reference to bankruptcy.

It occurred to Geithner that maybe Schwartz and his team were exaggerating the severity of the problem in hopes of securing a government bailout. Regardless, Bear was in bad shape. If the firm was really that close to filing Chapter 11, its life was probably over. If it accepted a cash infusion from the Fed, it was equally doomed, as that would no doubt worsen the already grave doubts among lenders and counterparties about whether Bear could survive.

Bear was still calculating its cash position and was in touch with potential suitors, Schwartz said. Since there was little he could do without more information, Geithner thanked him for the heads-up and asked him to keep in touch throughout the night. This situation had major ramifications for the markets and the economy, and he needed to get cracking on sorting those out.

Hoping to catch people before it got much later, Geithner quickly convened a conference call for all the major regulators.

Inside his home near the National Cathedral in Washington, Paulson was in a controlled rage. He and Geithner had conferred for months about Bear's tenuous position, and the godforsaken firm was in an unbelievable jam.

Paulson, who before running the Treasury had been CEO of Goldman, was well aware of the troubles his old industry was facing. He'd spent much of his time that month on the President's Working Group on Financial Markets, a coalition of regulators, central bankers, and cabinet members that was trying to come up with recommendations for better oversight of new mortgage loans, the rating agencies, and the securitization process, in which dealers took groups of home loans and packaged them into new securities for sale. He had also spent time on Wednesday helping his boss, President George W. Bush, prepare for an important speech on the capital markets that he would deliver in New York that Friday. It was a shaky time in the markets, and the president wanted to set the right tone.

During their discussions, Paulson and Bush had argued about one key aspect of the speech: what to say about the possibility of bailouts. Bush was leery of sending signals that his administration would bail out troubled securities firms, and wanted to convey that thinking in his speech. But Paulson thought he should leave his options open.

"Don't say that," he told Bush.

"Why?" the president had asked. "We're not going to have a bailout."

Paulson was adamant. He, too, was reluctant to leave open the possibility of a government rescue of any bank. But he knew the market was a volatile creature, and if a plummeting stock price or cash run was to push a firm to the breaking point, he didn't want the administration hamstrung by commitments it couldn't keep. "You don't want to help the banks until you do," he said. And sometime in the near future "you may need a bailout, as bad as that sounds."*

When he arrived at home that night, Paulson was so agitated, he wasn't sure what to do with himself. A conference call for regulators had been scheduled for 8:00, and he had some time to kill before his next update. He walked upstairs to his bedroom, and saw that the latest issue of *Sports Illustrated* had been placed on his bed. He grabbed it, lay down, and began paging through the basketball coverage.

At 8:00, the SEC staff dialed in from D.C., and Geithner and his top people were patched in from their offices and homes. Heading toward Capitol Hill when the phone rang, Federal Reserve governor Kevin Warsh pulled his Jeep Wrangler over to the side of the road so he could concentrate. Steel was in a similar position. He'd flown from Washington to New York that evening to surprise his youngest daughter at a dinner to celebrate her twenty-first birthday. But since landing around 6:00, he'd been waylaid in an airport conference room, talking on the phone while his wife and children ate dinner without him.

---

*Tony Fratto, a Bush White House spokesperson, said, "The president's conversations are confidential."

Geithner told the group he'd just heard from Schwartz. Bear's executives believed it was on the verge of bankruptcy, he explained. Unlike depository banks J.P. Morgan and Citigroup, which were regulated by the Fed, Bear was overseen by the SEC, which Geithner presumed had been keeping close tabs on its cash holdings. He wanted to know if the Commission staff agreed with Schwartz that bankruptcy was near. "Is that your judgment?" he asked.

Yes, replied Erik Sirri, the former finance professor who headed the SEC's division of trading and markets.

The Fed officials, who had been skeptical of Bear's position for days, were not surprised by the news. But the SEC's tone was an about-face. For weeks the Commission staff had appeared sanguine about Bear's situation, noting that its capital levels were higher than ever and that things seemed to be stable. It was lost on officials like Geithner and Warsh how their counterparts had missed the bigger picture until now.

SEC staffers, however, found themselves in a frustrating bind. As the chief regulator for U.S. investment banks, monitoring Bear and its cash positions was indeed their mandate. But there was a limit to how much advice they could give. Sure, Bear's leverage ratio now appeared far too high for comfort, but the Commission lacked the ability to demand any changes. Had the SEC approached Bear during the boom period of 2006 or 2007 and asked the company nicely to deleverage then, officials were relatively certain the firm would have told them to fuck off. Their participation in the SEC's investment-banking oversight program, after all, was voluntary, and some regulation was certainly better than none.

"Okay," said Geithner. "I'm getting my team to come back to the office so we can work through this."

"Let's schedule a conference call for the morning," one of the SEC staffers replied. "We're going to bed. Let us know if we can help." They felt there was little left to do now. If the Fed was going to lend money to Bear—and it was the only government entity with the power to do so—they certainly weren't going to tell the Commission about it.

The Prior Summer

The Fed had had its eye on Bear in August 2007. As with other pure investment banks, such as Goldman, Lehman Bros., and Morgan Stanley, the SEC was Bear's regulator of record; the Fed handled commercial banks like J.P. Morgan and Citigroup. But when the signs of a looming credit crisis had begun to emerge in 2007, it became clear that Bear was in trouble, and the SEC was behind the eight ball. Geithner and his team believed the time might come for them to step in.

Riding high on its year-end profits, Bear had sailed through the first couple of quarters of 2007. The firm had a huge mortgage business, and the bull run in housing was treating it well. Unsurprisingly, Bear's credit analysts remained upbeat on the housing sector, even as doubts about the health of subprime loans crept in.

That spring, Bear had an embarrassing tussle with one of its big clients. A prominent hedge fund manager, John Paulson, accused the firm of double-dealing in its handling of certain securities. Paulson was bearish on the subprime market and was buying credit-default swaps, or insurance policies, that would compensate him if subprime securities lost value. Bear sold the swaps, and had sold some to Paulson. But since the firm also packaged and serviced some of the very subprime securities that Paulson was betting would fall, he worried Bear might try to prop up those securities by renegotiating the home loans they contained to prevent them from going into default—a situation that would otherwise cause the securities to drop in value.

John Paulson had worked at Bear earlier in his career, and he knew the firm well. In addition to buying its swaps, he was among the prime-brokerage division's biggest clients. He managed about $12 billion altogether, a large hunk of which he kept in his Bear account. He knew the firm wouldn't want to piss him off.

He also knew its employees were capable of reckless behavior. At a Las Vegas industry conference early in the year, one of Bear's top mortgage traders had spoken out of turn. Over drinks with another hedge fund manager who happened to be a friend of Paulson's, the trader bragged about a plan to do exactly what Paulson feared: use Bear's unique rights as a servicer of mortgage-backed securities to help keep certain shaky homeowners out of default, thus preserving the value of the loans backing the securities and avoiding any big payouts to clients holding swaps.

Paulson had heard enough. Late that spring he had a series of heated exchanges with his contacts at Bear. Unsatisfied with their responses, he complained to the International Swaps and Derivatives Association as well as the SEC. He then took his complaints public. Bear was put on the defensive, and the SEC launched an investigation. Federal prosecutors in the Brooklyn office of the U.S. Attorney, where Bear's back-office operations were housed, soon took an interest as well.

Meanwhile, trouble was brewing on another front. One of the hedge funds in Bear's own money-management unit, Bear Stearns Asset Management, was struggling. Year to date, its performance had fallen 23 percent, and shocked investors were demanding their money back. But the fund's managers had borrowed heavily against their holdings, and didn't have the cash reserves to meet redemptions.

Early in June 2007, the matter was discussed by Bear's executive committee. Options were limited. Unless Bear itself lent money to the troubled fund, its managers would have to block investor redemptions—sending a hostile signal to its bread-and-butter clients—until they could raise more cash themselves. Executives decided to let them go their own way. Things would blow over, they felt.

During this time, the fund's managers, Ralph Cioffi and Matthew Tannin, purported to be as shocked as anybody at the bad results. They had invested primarily in high-quality assets that were ranked AAA by ratings agencies. Sure, they had some exposure to subprime mortgages through sophisticated securities known as CDOs, or collateralized debt obligations. But their risk models revealed those investments to be safe, and had generated positive returns for several years. In fact, the managers had never experienced a down month until now.

Cioffi, a two-decade Bear veteran and father of four, was beloved within the firm. A hardworking mortgage salesman, he had pleaded for the chance to open his own fund, and after a six-month trial that had led to impressive returns, Bear agreed. The High-Grade Structured Credit Strategies Fund, which had opened for business in the fall of 2003, claimed some of the firm's favored clients as investors. Returns had been so strong in the first three years that Cioffi had launched another, riskier sister fund, called the High-Grade Structured Credit Strategies Enhanced Leverage Fund. True to its name, the fund attempted to goose, or enhance, returns by upping the amount of leverage it employed, borrowing about $10 for every $1 it had in cold, hard cash or collateral. That was less leverage than an average Wall Street firm employed, but more than many of the better-managed hedge funds.

The riskier fund's lenders were a who's who of Wall Street, and now they smelled blood. A number of lenders, including J.P. Morgan, made margin calls on Cioffi's funds, and when he couldn't make good, they threw him into default. Hoping to monetize some of their assets, Cioffi and Tannin began a fire sale of the bonds they held, off-loading at least $8 billion into the markets in May and June. Still they couldn't keep up with investor and lender demands. The housing market, now saddled with a growing number of late payments and borrowers in default, was in freefall. Home prices were dropping, and investors were questioning the meaning of AAA.

By late June, they were being crushed. The Enhanced Leverage Fund was a lost cause, sunk by withering investments and unmanageable demands for cash. But there was still hope for the original fund, which was on the hook for less money. Bear authorized an emergency $3.2 billion loan to that fund, hoping to bail it out. Cioffi and his boss were relieved of their day-to-day operational duties, and Tom Marano, who understood mortgage securities better than any other executive, was called in to do triage.

But Marano could not get things under control. The combination of falling asset prices and a huge debt load made it impossible to pay creditors back. Late in July, he reluctantly filed for bankruptcy protection for both funds.

In August, market conditions turned hellacious. During the first week alone, a number of quantitative hedge funds, which rely on sophisticated mathematical predictions to make trades, sustained double-digit percentage losses. Securities firm stocks were getting hit, too. Bear had lost more than $50 per share since its spring high, and competitors like Lehman and Merrill were also getting crushed.

On Friday, August 3, Standard & Poor's confirmed what many investors and rival firms had come to believe. Cutting its outlook on Bear from stable to negative, the rating agency said in a statement that Bear's "reputation has suffered from the widely publicized problems of its managed hedge funds, leaving the company a potential target of litigation from investors who have suffered substantial losses." Bear fought back with its own release, saying its balance sheet was stable and healthy. That day, its stock hit a twelve-month low, and the cost of buying swaps to protect against a Bear default reached its highest multiple in years.

Bear executives then held a conference call to reassure the public. In fact, it did the opposite. Cayne called the market environment "extremely challenging," then left the room and didn't return in time for an investor's question. Molinaro, in an unguarded moment he would later rue, said that after twenty-two years in the business, "this is as bad as I've seen it in the fixed-income market." Upton's reassurances that Bear had halved its reliance on short-term funding since the beginning of the year had little effect. As the call wore on, the Dow began a downward slide that would leave it 280 points lower for the day, more than a 2 percent drop.

Unbeknownst to the public, Bear had already taken another step that would further depress confidence: It had sacked Cayne's heir apparent, Warren Spector. Cocksure and sometimes difficult to work with, Spector had made a lot of enemies within the firm. But the forty-nine-year-old former trader was also Bear's most competent operator, and he knew Bear's fixed-income division intimately. Much as some people disliked him, especially as his wealth grew and he spent more and more time at his plush home in Martha's Vineyard, Spector was one of the few Bear executives who could take hold of a pressing problem and make a quick judgment. It was unclear what the firm would do without him.

News of Spector's imminent departure leaked out late Friday, and the move was made official in a hastily convened Sunday board meeting. By then, Cayne and his team had already moved on. The SEC was on their tail, and would be monitoring the firm's movements daily for a long time to come.

9:00 P.M.

Inside 383 Madison, Gary Parr was still dialing for dollars. Next on his list was Chris Flowers, the billionaire buyout executive. Now fifty, Flowers had headed Goldman's financial institutions investment-banking group until 1998, when he'd left over a leadership dispute. Since then, his eponymous company had made successful investments in financial services companies in both Asia and the United States, bolstering his reputation for quick, smart deal making.

Flowers had flirted briefly with Bear the prior August. Tempted by the company's sagging stock price, he had sent a team to 383 to meet with senior managers in fixed income and discuss a possible investment. But the Bear participants had been turned off by the overture. They felt that Flowers was merely bottom-feeding, determining just how bad a position they were in so he could make other investment decisions.

Parr knew that, just like Dimon, Flowers could put together a quick deal. But there was something else he liked: the seal of approval that a respected private investor could bring to his struggling client. Maybe a move by Flowers would inject some confidence into clients and lenders, he thought.

Flowers was aboard his private jet somewhere over Canada when he got the call. "Chris, there's an important opportunity here and things are moving very quickly," Parr told him. "I'm working with Bear Stearns."

Parr briefly explained the situation, saying that an immediate investment or quick turnaround deal was going to be essential.

"How quickly do you want to move?" asked Flowers. "How much capital is going to be needed here?"

Parr said he was thinking about something in the low billions of dollars. With Bear's stock price so depressed, the firm had a market capitalization of $12 billion or so, he said, and a cash injection of $3 billion to $5 billion could make a world of difference in shoring up market confidence. J.P. Morgan, he added, was also in the mix.

Flowers promised to think about it. He was intrigued, but concerned about the competition from J.P. Morgan. If the large bank was interested, there was no way Flowers could compete. His boutique firm lacked the balance sheet and the manpower to match his opponent. But if J.P. Morgan was on the fence, Flowers might consider going ahead. The best way to decide, he figured, was to tackle this head-on.

Flowers called Dimon, who by now had abandoned his birthday

party and retreated to his Upper East Side apartment. The buyout executive explained his situation. He'd gotten a call that night from Bear Stearns, he said, and he understood Dimon had, too. It sounded like there could be an attractive opportunity there, but only for a fast-moving buyer. Was J.P. Morgan going to bite? Flowers asked.

"I don't know what we're going to do, but you should do whatever you want," Dimon told him. J.P. Morgan might be interested in a deal, he said, but it was far too early to commit to anything. Okay, thought Flowers, this actually might be worth some time. He began canvassing his own private-equity team to see who could be available for some quick due diligence the next day.

By then Dimon had spoken to Schwartz as well.

"Let's do something," the Bear CEO had told him. It was too short notice for a wholesale purchase of Bear, he knew, but the firm wouldn't open on Friday without a quick cash infusion. He asked Dimon to consider providing a $25 billion line of credit. The J.P. Morgan chief agreed to look into it.

Having hung up with Schwartz, Dimon focused on tracking down Steve Black, his right arm on a deal of this nature. On vacation with his family in Anguilla, Black, the cochief of J.P. Morgan's investment bank and an old ally of Dimon's from their shared days at Citi, had left his cell phone back at the hotel while he dined out with his wife. Dimon needed to figure out where he was eating and find the phone number of the restaurant.

As he waited for J.P. Morgan's team to show up, Molinaro was growing increasingly jittery. This was a disaster of profound proportions, he thought. He just couldn't believe what a crisis had befallen Bear. The SEC and the Fed had been posted, and he was crossing his fingers that an investment or a merger would come together. But what if it didn't?

He wasn't sure what a Chapter 11 filing would entail. What if Bear didn't have enough money to operate the next day? How much would it need anyway? Could the firm still open? What about the transactions it did with other firms and with clients—would Bear be dealing in bad faith if its cash position was so deeply compromised?

Alone in his corner office, Molinaro called Schwartz and Metrick, who were up on the forty-second floor, to ask what the status was of retaining a bankruptcy lawyer. He wanted someone immediately, not in a few hours. The three had been discussing whom to hire for half the night already. "I need a bankruptcy lawyer here, like, now!" Molinaro bellowed at Metrick.

Bear's outside counsel, the crusty deals lawyer Dennis Block, had rushed up from his offices at Cadwalader, Wickersham & Taft shortly after the big meeting. Sensing the urgency, he called his partner in the bankruptcy litigation department, Bruce Zirinsky, and asked him to join them. While they were waiting for his arrival, Block talked to Schwartz and Metrick about other options. Bear had been arguing for months that the Fed should open the discount window to investment banks, but there was no sign yet that the government would do so, and the firm needed a cash infusion as soon as possible.

The group discussed the possibilities, including J.P. Morgan and Warren Buffett. After his bruising experience with Salomon Brothers in the 1980s and 1990s, the Omaha billionaire had indicated he would never again put his money into an investment bank. But Buffett had friends at Bear, and surely he was concerned about the risk its failure posed to the entire financial system.

This was the issue most bothering Geithner and Paulson that night. Bear wouldn't fail in a vacuum, they knew. The crisis of confidence among lenders and clients would likely spread to the next most vulnerable firm—be it Lehman Brothers or Merrill Lynch. Both firms were thought to be overexposed to the housing crisis, Lehman had its large commercial real-estate portfolio as well as its sprawling mortgage-origination and packaging activities, and Merrill was invested heavily in enormous underwater investments in CDOs. If skeptical investors and frightened customers and lenders were able to sink Bear, a series of dominoes could fall after it—potentially taking down most or all of Wall Street.

Paulson was envisaging a 1,000- to 2,000-point drop in the Dow if Bear's meltdown were to have a ripple effect—a positively catastrophic outcome that would erase billions of dollars of wealth. In their discussion with aides and with each other, he and Geithner began using a dramatic analogy: They couldn't "spray enough foam on the runway" to prevent this jetliner from crashing.

Bear's collapse wouldn't be limited to the financial services firms, either. A bankrupt firm would dump a plethora of troubled securities into the market. These included mortgage-backed securities, corporate loans, and a large swath of derivatives, like credit-default swaps. Amid the mortgage downturn and lending dry-up, bids for many such securities were already low, but adding thousands of bits of new inventory to a market with few sellers would only depress the prices further, harming other banks and funds that were already struggling to sell the same sorts of items.

Zirinsky finally arrived. It was well into the evening, and the Asian markets were already open, the lawyers realized. They wondered aloud whether they should issue a press release to reveal Bear's liquidity problems. What if the firm couldn't open its doors on Friday? Molinaro's question was answered: New York state law mandated that if a firm didn't have the money to pay its employees, it couldn't open for business.

From his office, Molinaro called his wife, Lisa, who was at home in New Canaan, Connecticut, with two of their three children. The eldest, Danielle, was in college in Boston. "We've got major problems," Molinaro said, adding that he'd be staying late.

Bear had to prepare for the worst, and with nearly five hundred subsidiary units, someone had to figure out which would be asking for Chapter 11 protection and which could be left alone. Zirinsky was soon joined by dozens of legal associates. Fanning out over Molinaro's conference room, the legal library, and other large offices on the sixth floor, the legal team scrambled to assess Bear's balance sheet. Bankruptcy required debtor-in-possession financing—money to see it through the period during which it was in Chapter 11 bankruptcy protection—in the form of cash or assets. The trouble was, it was hard to know how many billions of dollars Bear would need in order to cover every eventuality—further demands for prime-brokerage client cash to be returned, for example. Moreover, many of Bear's valuable assets were sitting in the hands of its trading partners, who were holding the bonds and other securities as collateral. The lawyers wondered how they could free those assets for Bear's use. Could the firm possibly win a court injunction to force the other firms to hand that collateral over?

Pizzas and greasy Chinese food had been spread out in Molinaro's conference room, and hungry employees from other floors were drifting in and out to grab a bite. The presence of so many bankruptcy lawyers was making them nervous.

In response to lingering questions about the firm's cash position, Upton had put together an updated legal-pad reckoning with more solid numbers, which he had copied and passed around to the group from the 6:00 meeting. There, Bear's problem was laid out in black-and-white chicken scrawl. Having started the week with a total of $18.1 billion in cash, the firm had simply hemorrhaged money. Fixed-income financing had eaten up $2.5 billion. About $900 million of commercial paper loans had disappeared and was all but certain not to be renewed. Hedge funds and other prime-brokerage customers had wired out $13.9 billion in cash.

On the positive side, Bear had taken out $1.9 billion in bank loans. Payments owed to Bear from foreign-exchange trades were set to bring in $900 million. From the 15c3-3 account, $555 million had been removed, cash that would be replaced as early as Friday. All told, Bear now had $5.655 billion in cash—a number that was rewritten several times in ballpoint pen and circled by Upton—but it owed Citi $2.4 billion of that, leaving Bear with a grand total of a little more than $3 billion.

Ensconced in his office upstairs, Schwartz realized he needed to call a board meeting. Much had changed since the last directors' meeting, and board members would need to know about the bankruptcy threat.

Schwartz asked his team to alert directors to the need for a late-night gathering. Quite a few lived outside New York, so it would have to be done over the telephone.

Bear's lead independent director, Vincent Tese, was having dinner with Fred Salerno—a fellow director and good friend—at an Italian restaurant in Jupiter, Florida, when his cell phone rang. He looked down and saw from the caller identification number that it was Molinaro, who had owed him a call since 2:30 that afternoon.

"This ain't good news," Tese said as he rose from the table.

Outside the restaurant, he talked to the CFO, who explained what Bear was dealing with. Tese shook his head as he returned to the table. "We're going to have a board call," he told Salerno. They quickly finished their meal and returned to their respective homes.

Back at his apartment in Palm Beach, Tese pondered the situation. He had had a sinking feeling all week, and a few days ago he had called Molinaro. "Sam, what's going on?" Tese asked. He had seen the hysterical CNBC reports about Bear's trouble trading and read the headlines about its cash problems. Molinaro had replied that he didn't know. "Our liquidity position has never been stronger," the CFO had said.

Based on what he knew of the firm's condition, Tese was inclined to agree. Bear had a sterling reputation for risk management, and the firm's computer models had always indicated that its risk-taking activities were well within acceptable limits.

Paul Friedman was pacing the halls, now bathed in artificial light as darkness descended over the city. He had briefed the "death squad"— his term for the bankruptcy lawyers—on the dozen or so Bear subsidiaries with which he was familiar, but had left them to sort out the other 450.

His anxiety was driven by his passion for the place. A kind-faced, balding father of two, Friedman, who had been hired on a lark after meeting Bear's head of operations in a hallway, could barely remember the accounting job he'd had before joining Bear. Over the course of the twenty-six years he'd been with the company, he had benefited from the firm's success, eventually building a spacious home in tony Scarsdale, New York, developing an avid golf habit, and taking his wife on European vacations. He had also come to love Bear's rough-and-tumble culture and especially its lack of hierarchy. If you had an issue with how a program was managed, you'd soon be put in charge of it. "We're not big on titles," he liked to say.

Hoping for a little peace, he went up to his seventh-floor office, just off the mortgage-backed trading floor that had long been at the heart of Bear. Sitting at his desk, Friedman noticed an e-mail from his buddy Bruce Geismar, Bear's head of operations. It was time stamped 8:35. "How bad is it?" read the subject line.

"Very. End of the world bad," Friedman typed back a couple of minutes later.

"Where are you?" replied Geismar, who had gone home earlier. "Were repo lines pulled?"

"In office," wrote Friedman. "Rp isn't the problem, free credits, cp and bank lines are," he explained, referring to client cash that had flown out the door, commercial paper, and loans from banks that were now looking like an endangered species.

About an hour later, Friedman e-mailed his wife, Susie, who was at home in Westchester. "Still here," the note said.

Eighty blocks downtown, Geithner was now in the New York Fed's grand offices on Liberty Street, surrounded by staff. They were bracing themselves for a Bear bankruptcy, hoping to think through the implications before they came to pass.

Between calls, Geithner phoned Schwartz. The Bear CEO had told the regulator he was reaching out to potential acquirers, and Geithner wanted an update. "What have you heard from J.P. Morgan?" he asked.

"Well, I really haven't heard," Schwartz said.

"Why don't you call them back," Geithner said.

He had already spoken to J.P. Morgan himself.

"We can't buy this thing tonight," Dimon had told Geithner shortly after he'd heard from Schwartz.

"Go in and look at the thing, and let's talk," Geithner said. Something had to be done. He was eager to know what J.P. Morgan was finding.

Steve Black, cohead of J.P. Morgan's enormous investment bank, had been looking forward to a real vacation. Since the credit crunch had first ballooned the prior spring, Black had had several holidays either canceled or interrupted by business, and this time he was hoping to wind down properly.

He was at a restaurant in Anguilla with his wife, Debbie, when a man from the kitchen walked over to the table. "Oh, shit," Black muttered as he approached.

"Are you Mr. Black?" asked the man. Black nodded. "Mr. Dimon is on the phone for you," the man responded. He pointed toward the kitchen.

Black walked back toward the kitchen, where a team of cooks was busy preparing food. One of them was holding a phone. "I think that's for me," Black said.

Dimon was on the other end. He had gotten calls from Schwartz and Parr, he explained, and Bear was going to go out of business unless they found some kind of solution. Dimon needed a team that could look at Bear's books that night. Black was needed back by morning, at the latest.

Black hung up and headed back to his hotel room, where he called John Hogan, his chief of risk, and a few others. His cochief of the investment bank, Bill Winters, was probably asleep in London, so Black figured he'd wait a few hours to call.

Matt Zames, who ran a number of the firm's trading divisions, including foreign exchange and mortgages, had just nodded off in his northern New Jersey home when he was jarred awake by a call. You need to come in, Hogan told him. Bear was in desperate shape and the bank was considering making a spur-of-the-moment investment.

10:30 P.M.

Around 10:30 P.M., Molinaro and Schwartz gathered in one of the twelfth-floor dining rooms to address directors. Lawyers had taken over the conference rooms on the sixth floor, and the executives had too many people amassed to sit in a private office. Greenberg had returned from a dinner meeting, and Frank "Nick" Nickell, another director, who ran the small brokerage firm Kelso & Company, had come to 383 to participate in person.

Tese and Salerno dialed in from Florida, and most others joined from their respective homes. Cayne was patched in from Detroit. He was there for a national bridge tournament, and when Molinaro had called his hotel room to alert him to the meeting, Cayne's wife, Patricia, had said that he was downstairs playing. Cayne had to be interrupted, Molinaro said. He and Schwartz had concluded that they could not proceed without Bear's chairman.

Schwartz and Molinaro began by explaining what had transpired in the two days since the CNBC appearance. Now that they were nearly out of cash, bankruptcy was a real possibility, they said. J.P. Morgan was in talks with Bear, they added, and a team of people from the bank was en route to see what they could do that night.

"This is a liquidity issue, not a capital issue," Schwartz told the group.

Bear and its banker, Gary Parr, were doing their level best to come up with a deal for Bear, Schwartz said, but a private-sector solution was not assured. "You can't open your doors unless you can live up to your obligations," Schwartz said, "and so unless we get some assurance from the Fed that we can do that, we're not going to open." Indeed, another bankruptcy expert, from Skadden, Arps, Slate, Meagher & Flom, had just walked in signaling that, despite Bear's hope for a deal, the bankruptcy proceedings were moving fast.

Like other directors, Cayne was surprisingly subdued. The situation was awful, but there wasn't much that could be done about it until a deal or a bailout emerged. Without a rescue, bankruptcy was inevitable. All the board could do was hope and pray. There was no point in taking a vote.

Schwartz explained what he was asking J.P. Morgan for: a $25 billion secured line of credit to help see it through the short-term problems. Bear would do whatever it could to make that happen and avoid Chapter 11, he said.

Back in his Palm Beach apartment, Tese knew Bear was in deep trouble. But something in his gut told him a bailout would happen. He'd been New York's superintendent of banks for a number of years, and he'd seen banks on the brink of failure before. Regulators didn't like to see financial institutions simply fail. Something, he felt, would be done.

11:00 P.M.

Mala Greenberger, the senior Bear lawyer who advised Green's repo desk, walked into Marano's office.

The burly mortgage trader was lost in thought. On the wall behind his desk hung his collection of guitars that had been played and signed by stars like the Allman Brothers, Aerosmith, and Counting Crows. Marano even had body art that reflected his tastes. In 1995, when Jerry Garcia, the Grateful Dead's lead guitarist, had died, Marano got an image of the Dead's *Steal Your Face* album cover—a skull bifurcated by a lightning bolt—tattooed to his right shoulder. "I wasn't even drunk," Marano would joke when asked about it.

Marano's love of music, especially "jam bands" like the Allman Brothers and the Grateful Dead, was well known within Bear. He had had some good times at concerts with his coworkers. Every year, he and another trader led a big group of Bear employees and customers to the Allman Brothers spring concert at the Beacon Theatre on Seventy-fourth Street. It was always a raucous show, with plenty of marijuana smoke hovering in the air—prompting everyone to come home smelling like they'd spent the evening at a fraternity party.

By 2007, most of Bear's enormous mortgage team turned out, plus clients and friends, and the size of the group had soared to about one thousand—more than one-third of the Beacon's seating capacity. The evening started with a big party at Tavern on the Green, the tourist mecca in Central Park, and continued after the concert at a local bar. This year, the band was scheduled to play again in May, and Bear had bought another block of a thousand or so tickets and planned another blowout set of parties.

But on the evening of March 13, the Allman Brothers concert was a distant notion as Greenberger stood in the doorway. She gave Marano a grim look. "It doesn't look good, does it," she finally said.

"No," Marano replied. "I think it's over."

A fixture at Bear since 1983, the bearded, pudgy father of three was a hothead who tended to speak his mind. For many years everyone had listened to him as profits rose in the all-powerful fixed-income division where he worked, driven largely by Bear's enormous mortgage unit. Marano, a Columbia University history major who had a large home in Madison, New Jersey, and a wine cellar full of great vintages, was one of the best-paid people at the company, and for good reason, he felt. Now, after a few bruising days in the stock market, his net worth had fallen by nearly half.

"Yeah, I saw the same procession walk in," Greenberger said, referring to the Cadwalader bankruptcy lawyers.

"Yeah," said Marano. "They looked like the undertakers."

11:30 P.M.

Matt Zames had been down this road before. He had started his career at Long-Term Capital Management in the winter of 1994, shortly after college. There he witnessed firsthand what could happen when a bunch of shortsighted executives didn't manage their risk properly. In September 1998, when Long-Term's massive losses had prompted an emergency meeting at the New York Fed, Wall Street's top players had cobbled together an eleventh-hour bailout of the fund, hoping to stave off collateral damage to the financial system. Even Lehman Brothers, then besieged by leery lenders and negative back talk about the health of its business, chipped in $100 million—substantially less than the $300 million most other firms had contributed, but a meaningful number, given the firm's straits. Bear, of course, had given nothing.

When he arrived in Midtown, Zames had the car drop him at J.P. Morgan's building on Park Avenue. He didn't even want his driver to see him go into Bear's offices, for fear that inside information about his company's talks with the troubled firm would leak into the marketplace.

By the time he reached the sixth floor it was after midnight. His team was huddled with a group of Bear managers in one of the conference rooms. Zames had one question for the Bear team: How much cash and collateral did it have on hand?

Upton and Friedman began explaining. The firm had about $3 billion of unencumbered cash, they believed, but it also had collateral it could use the next day to raise money: high-quality corporate bonds in Europe, various stock holdings there and in the United States, some lower-quality mortgage bonds. Altogether, Upton estimated, Bear could come up with at least $7 billion using those securities, and maybe as much as $10 billion if they were lucky.

His list of collateral securities in hand, Upton offered to explain in greater detail. Was the J.P. Morgan group interested in hearing more about the securities they wanted to pledge? he asked. If so, Bear had CUSIPs, or identifying codes, for the stocks and bonds they were discussing.

Zames shook his head. "That's not going to be necessary," he told them. "This whole thing is fucked. We need to call someone very senior, because you will not last the day. Where's the Fed?"

He and one of his deputies found an empty office and called their contacts at the Fed. Zames told the officials that Bear was facing a very similar situation to the one LTCM had found itself in a decade ago. If an immediate funding solution wasn't found, he explained, there was no way that Bear could do business on Friday. The officials replied that they would see what they could do, and the J.P. Morgan team retreated to their offices across the street to discuss things further.

Marano returned home to New Jersey sometime after midnight and went straight to the wine cellar. Standing in front of the early 1980s

Bordeaux bottles, he searched for a Château Margaux from 1983—the year he had started working full time at Bear. Finding none, he had to settle instead for a 1982 bottle.

A couple of glasses later, he turned in for the night. His wife, Amy, was asleep, and he didn't bother to wake her up. For her own protection, he had warned her earlier that week not to ask him any questions about what was happening at Bear. "I don't know what's going to happen," he had said, "but it looks like it's going to be really bad."

FRIDAY
March 14, 2008

2:00 A.M.

At 383, the hand-wringing continued.

Bear treasurer Bob Upton spent half the night handling calls with officials and staffers from the Fed and the SEC, giving updates on all aspects of Bear's balance sheet and what assets the firm thought it could pledge. The key, of course, was whether J.P. Morgan would come through with something. But there was radio silence from across the street. Molinaro stayed close to his corner office, hoping for an encouraging call.

Pat Lewis, his nerves frayed, went home to lie down for a while and get a change of clothes. He had done all he could for the evening, and his head was starting to hurt. Things were changing so fast he could hardly keep track. During his one down moment, he had called his father in Naples, Florida. "It's been a crazy night," Lewis told him. A retired small-business owner, Lewis's dad was one of the few people he could confide in who knew something about the business world. The deputy treasurer kept the details to himself, knowing he worked in a sensitive part of the business that dealt with a lot of nonpublic information. But Lewis's rest was short-lived. Only an hour or two after getting home, he got an urgent call from a colleague to return to 383. He was back by three o'clock

Shuttling between six and his seventh floor office, Friedman was fielding concerned e-mails all night. Jeff Mayer, one of his pals and the cohead of fixed income, e-mailed at 2:00 A.M. "Call when you know the outcome," Mayer wrote. "I will be in at 6:30 A.M." Okay, Friedman thought. To Mayer, he wrote, "We're a long way from getting anything done."

By 3:30 A.M., the J.P. Morgan team had headed back to its own building across the street. John Hogan, the risk officer, had arrived from his home in the suburbs to find Matt Zames, the senior trader, and a colleague in his office. Bear's situation was a disaster, they told him.

Dimon was still in his Uptown apartment manning the phones, and Black, still in Anguilla, awaited the corporate jet to fly him back to headquarters. After alerting his closest colleagues that he'd be needing their help to vet Bear, he had called his public-relations chief, Kristin Lemkau, at her downtown apartment, waking her up in the middle of the night. "There's a good chance that Bear Stearns could go out of business," he had told her. J.P. Morgan was looking at a bunch of options, he said, and "I need you in early tomorrow morning." She was toweling off her wet hair at 4:15 A.M. when Hogan called. "Are you coming in?" he asked. "We need your help with a press release." She quickly pulled her clothes on and headed uptown, where Hogan, Zames, and J.P. Morgan general counsel Steve Cutler were now waiting.

At about the same time, Friedman e-mailed his wife, Susie. "There's an outside chance that JP Morgan Chase will bail us out," he wrote. "They have about 3 more hours to decide and I make it less than 50/50 that they will. If they do, we get to announce to the world that they've agreed to backstop us and we live to the weekend, at which point we probably give the firm away to them."

"If they say no," he added, "we're declaring bankruptcy and I really can't believe we came to this."

At his house in the preppy Georgetown section of Washington, D.C., Fed governor Kevin Warsh was wide awake. His last call with Geithner had ended sometime after 2:00, and now he was hashing things out with Schwartz.

An investment banker at Morgan Stanley before he'd joined the government in 2002, the thirty-seven-year-old Warsh spoke Schwartz's language. They had come to know each other well in recent years, and the young Fed governor respected Schwartz's knowledge of the capital markets. He was good at objectively considering an array of options, then making what he considered the best possible suggestions. Because of that, Warsh asked for his point of view from time to time.

He had also brokered Schwartz's first meeting with Geithner some months before. Federal Reserve Chairman Ben Bernanke, a former Princeton professor still relatively new to his job, had made a point of visiting nearly every single Fed branch to talk with local executives and bankers. (In Atlanta, Warsh had filled in for Bernanke the one time he had been forced to cancel a trip because of business overseas.) Although Bernanke had passed through New York for those meetings, he had not attended the same one as Schwartz.

The officials found Bear's CEO to be sharp and broad-minded, considering that he now effectively ran a firm whose primary business—the sales and trading of stocks and bonds—had long been outside his purview in investment banking. Unlike his predecessor, Cayne, who was not interested in having academic discussions or hobnobbing with regulators, Schwartz moved easily among fellow businessmen and government officials and could talk on a wide range of topics far beyond mergers and acquisitions.

Lean and stylish, Warsh cut an unusual figure for a Fed governor. A native of upstate New York who had attended Harvard Law School, he was married to Jane Lauder, a granddaughter of the famous cosmetics executive Estée Lauder. The couple was often spotted in the New York and Washington society pages, and Lauder, who ran the Origins natural-product label of her grandmother's sprawling company, was a fixture on the fashion-show circuit.

At Morgan Stanley, Warsh had become executive director of the mergers-and-acquisitions business within the investment bank. Then, in 2002, he moved to Washington to work as an economic adviser to President Bush. He participated in the President's Working Group on the Financial Markets, and also dealt frequently with the regulatory agencies.

Warsh's age alone made him something of an anomaly at the Fed, where many of the staff had worked for decades, and appointees sometimes as long. But his approachability and knowledge of Wall Street at a time when securities firms were on their heels soon made him indispensable to associates like Vice Chairman Don Kohn and Bernanke, who had no industry experience.

Sipping a Diet Coke in his home office on this long night, Warsh thought about his last conversation with Schwartz. He could tell that the CEO was anxious. They talked through the possibilities that Bear was facing: bankruptcy, a bailout, or a third-party investment. Schwartz was concerned about both employees and shareholders. He didn't want Bear's fourteen thousand workers turned out onto the street without so much as a day's warning. And that wasn't his only fear. In addition to the deep-pocketed fund managers and corporate executives who had invested in Bear, a large minority of the company's shares were held by more junior-level employees. Some were secretaries with relatively small salaries or lifers close to retirement. If their holdings were wiped out, the loss of work would be doubly devastating.

Warsh understood. But as a Fed official, he couldn't worry too much about Bear and its team's collective concerns. The U.S. economy was on shaky ground here. Housing prices had cratered, markets had declined, and financial firms were under increasing pressure, curtailing the credit they would normally extend to American businesses. Warsh and his colleagues had to balance all those concerns against the short-term problems of one relatively small investment bank. Their job was to mitigate systemic risk.

He wasn't the only sleepless government official. After several hours of running point on his team's research into the larger impact of a Bear bankruptcy, Geithner had left the office for a nearby hotel around 1:00 A.M., hoping to catch a little sleep before the next round of calls. A couple of hours later, his ringing phone jolted him awake.

It was a staff member from his office, calling to report on the team's findings. The consequences would be widespread, the staffer said.

A career public servant who served the U.S. Treasury abroad in India, Japan, and East Africa, the forty-six-year-old New York Fed bank president prided himself on being rational. Gregarious, hard-working, and blunt when he needed to be, Geithner was the kind of presence that could reassure both staffers and corporate executives. His mentors included Henry Kissinger and Robert Rubin, the former Goldman head who became Treasury secretary under President Bill Clinton. Geithner's board of advisers at the New York Fed included heavy hitters like Dimon and Merrill Lynch chief John Thain.

Farther below the radar, Geithner had a handful of money managers and other executives he kept in touch with by phone during business hours, polling them on how the trading day was going and what issues they saw in the markets. One of his pals was Lee Sachs, a former Bear trader who now ran his own hedge fund, Mariner Investments. For a number of years, Geithner, Sachs, and former Treasury Secretary Lawrence Summers had traveled together to Bradenton, Florida, for tennis lessons at the renowned Nick Bollettieri Tennis Academy.

Geithner's approach to crises was pragmatic: Think through the choices, be as cool-headed as possible, and decide on the best option. Key to that, he felt, was getting people focused on the realistic options from a very early stage—not allowing them to chase down fantasy scenarios that had little chance of bearing out. Among colleagues at the Fed, he was infamous for lacing his bearish views on situations with the occasional zinger. "I don't mean to be dark, but . . ." was the introduction he often gave to a doomsday scenario he was about to describe. "A bad deal is better than no deal" was another favorite saying. Some associates joked that Geithner was so predisposed to seeing the dark side of things that his expression could grow pained even while talking about the weather.

Geithner knew that when it came to the securities industry executives he dealt with, putting the focus on practical possibilities was easier said than done. CEOs like Schwartz and Lehman chief Dick Fuld, for instance, had spent decades building businesses—thirty-two years in Schwartz's case and thirty-nine in Fuld's—and the companies were a huge part of their identities. That meant that ego sometimes got in the way of a good decision, even if it was fueled by the admirable intention to make a company succeed.

Tonight, as he and his staffer talked through the ramifications of a Chapter 11 filing, Geithner was worried about several things. One was the secured-funding market, in which banks and brokerages made loans to one another that were backed by assets like real estate, Treasury bonds, or cash. If Bear were to fail, its dozens of lenders would be stuck with billions of dollars in unpaid bills, potentially raising grave questions about the soundness of future borrowers. That meant that the next weakest links—probably Lehman and Merrill—could find themselves in the same position that Bear had in a matter of days.

He was also worried about the disruptions a Bear failure might cause to the derivatives market, an arena that comprises securities tied to underlying assets like stocks and bonds. *Derivative* is a general word that applies to everything from stock options to commodities, like gold and pork bellies; it consists simply of a bilateral, or two-party, contract. But the last several years had brought a slew of innovations to the market—perhaps most notably, the $46 trillion market for credit-default swaps, the insurance policies that paid the buyer money if the entity he or she was insuring failed to pay back its debt.

Swaps covered a variety of default risks, from large companies like Bear and Morgan Stanley to obscure pieces of mortgage-backed securities tied to home loans generated by specific mortgage lenders. Their prices fluctuated from minute to minute, and the protection purchased could cover a range of time frames. A standard bet was to buy swaps to pay out if an entity defaulted on $10 million of its debt at any time during a five-year period. But some swaps were even longer term, covering the entire maturity of, say, a thirty-year mortgage loan. Because their time frames tended to be long, swaps and their buyers and sellers were especially dependent on knowing that the party on the other end of the transaction was going to be in business for many years to come.

Geithner wondered if the companies whose job it was to finalize, or "settle," completed trades could even handle the sheer volume of a Bear closeout. The firm's failure would doubtless dump hundreds of millions of dollars in mortgage-backed securities, insurance policies against debt defaults by other companies, and countless other products into the open market at a time when prices for homes and bonds tied to their prices were falling precipitously.

Right now, he had no answers. It was time to bring in the government's best minds to try to hammer out a solution.

4:45 A.M.

Forty-five minutes ahead of schedule, the Fed officials, Paulson, and Steel began another call.

The Fed chairman, who needed to be available anytime, anyplace, had an open telephone line he could call twenty-four hours a day and have other parties patched through. Sitting at the kitchen table inside his Capitol Hill home, Bernanke dialed in, and the others went through a phone tree of passcodes and identifiers to join him on the line.

Bernanke that morning was in Socratic mode, grilling his associates for answers to the many questions. "What do we know? What do we think we know? What are our options?" he asked the group. "What's the state of any private-sector discussions?"

Geithner and Warsh, who had been in touch with Dimon and

Schwartz throughout the night, relayed the facts they had gathered. After a brutal couple of days in the marketplace, Bear had some $3 billion on hand, and only limited confidence in its ability to refresh its day-to-day financing in the morning.

"How confident are we that they can open?" asked Bernanke.

Not as confident as we'd like to be, replied the officials. If the past week had been any indication, Bear was in for another bad bruising. When these things happen, the officials pointed out, they happen fast.

Paulson chimed in. A financial crisis wasn't over, he believed, until you lost a couple of institutions you expected to lose and at least one institution you didn't expect to lose. Bear, with its lack of international operations and overdependence on the mortgage business, had long been vulnerable, he felt, and the fact that it was now on the hot seat suggested that the U.S. financial sector was at the start of a new period of turbulence. Somehow the government had to get Bear to the weekend, he said.

Privately, though, Paulson was dubious. Bear had been in a bad spot for a number of months, he knew, and there had been ample opportunity for buyers to snap up the firm at a distressed price. If no one had surfaced yet, they were unlikely to do so now.

Discussion turned to acquirers. There was good news and bad news there. J.P. Morgan might be interested in purchasing Bear. But given the short time frame, it had been unable to consider an overnight deal. Morgan would need the weekend to conduct the due diligence.

Bear, meanwhile, was hoping for a cash infusion. Dismayed that they couldn't borrow directly from the Fed, executives there had asked repeatedly for an opening of the discount window or some other form of relief. Now they were hoping, one last time, that the government would make an exception. It was their only hope for survival.

Bernanke addressed the subject of bankruptcy. "Can they open for business if they file?" he asked.

Not in New York State, was the answer.

The implications of Bear's travails were hitting the Fed chairman hard. It was possible, he thought, to be adequately capitalized under securities laws and still face a bank run. Even if federal regulators thought you looked okay, in other words, you could still be out of business overnight.

A scholar of the Great Depression, Bernanke's thoughts turned to Credit-Anstalt, the Austrian bank that had gone bankrupt in 1931. Hoping to stabilize their teetering economy by giving confidence to bank customers, the country's central bankers had guaranteed Credit-Anstalt's deposits—assuring the public that even if the bank went out of business, the government would ensure that they didn't lose their savings. Their move led to problems with Austria's currency, and created a sense of panic around Europe as the crisis spread.

One of Credit-Anstalt's disadvantages, Bernanke recalled, was that it had absorbed a number of smaller, weaker banks that had failed earlier in the downturn. Large and secure as it appeared, Credit-Anstalt could not take on all the liabilities of those other banks without taking a hit itself.

It struck the Fed chairman as a cautionary tale. Assuming that Bear could make it to the weekend, the question of who acquired it would become crucial. Bernanke didn't want a shaky Bear to be purchased by a seemingly healthier, larger firm, only to then see Bear's toxic assets topple its acquirer.

Geithner laid out several options. The riskiest was to let Bear file Chapter 11, providing enough government cash to other needy banks to enable the markets to run. The alternative was to give Bear a "bridge to the weekend," or a short-term loan. If the Fed took the latter course, its officials would have to decide whether or not to issue a statement of support for the firm—a step that might help soothe the nerves of a terrified public market.

The Fed officials worried about setting a precedent that it would bail out poorly run banks that hit the skids. But the effects of a Bear failure were potentially catastrophic. Of particular concern was a slice of the market that Fed researchers had of late been spending quite a bit of time on: the more than $2 trillion "tri-party repo market." This was the formal name for the overnight loan market on which Bear and other investment banks were so dependent. It was fueled by funding from entities like Fidelity Investments, which would provide short-term cash to recipients like Bear on a daily basis.

Caught between the Fidelitys and Bears of the world were the custodians, or clearing firms, that actually held the collateral underpinning the loans. Those middlemen, Bank of New York Mellon and J.P. Morgan, relieved the lender and borrower of the administrative burdens of handling the day-to-day transactions. But they also took on risks. If Bear, for instance, were unable to pay back its loan from Fidelity at the end of the day, J.P. Morgan would be on the hook for the loan money, and the collateral it held might have deteriorated in value, sticking it with losses. Moreover, if J.P. Morgan and BONY were burned more than once by transactions that lost them money, they might refuse to act as middlemen at all, potentially grinding the tri-party lending process to a halt and harming an array of large Wall Street brokerages that depended on the system.

"We need to get to the weekend," Bernanke said. Others concurred. "We really should do something to help," said Paulson.

5:30 A.M.

Before dawn on Friday, things were eerily quiet at Bear. Even Parr had gone home, and others were wishing they could. Still spread out across various sixth-floor offices, Block and Zirinsky's legal teams were working away. Block feared that a bankruptcy filing could mean chaos in the markets.

The tension on the sixth floor was growing palpable. Then, sometime after 5:00, there was news. Bear's general counsel got an e-mail from his counterpart at J.P. Morgan, Steve Cutler, saying to keep an eye out for an update—soon.

"Absolute torture," Paul Friedman wrote in a follow-up e-mail to Jeff Mayer, the cohead of fixed income. Mayer was en route from his home in New Jersey.

Around 5:30, Friedman walked over to the Manhattan Athletic Club to take a shower. He did not belong to the Bear gym. As he stepped out and grabbed a towel, still bleary-eyed, he spotted someone he knew from the charity circuit. "Paul, how are you?" the other man said. Foggy from his long night, Friedman couldn't remember the man's name. "Uh, yeah," he muttered, rushing off to get dressed. He couldn't worry about pleasantries at a time like this, and anything more than a brief conversation might lead something confidential to slip out.

Back on the sixth floor, Bear's public-relations team had arrived. An intern had been sent out to buy coffee and pastries from a nearby Dunkin' Donuts. Molinaro, Upton, and a handful of others were sitting around. After the most exhausting night they had ever endured, the group was operating on sheer adrenaline, and the gallows humor was in full force. "We need a Hail Mary pass, but we don't have any receivers," someone joked. There was tentative laughter. All they could do was wait.

6:00 A.M.

Back on the Fed conference call, there was a brief discussion of another option: an industry bailout. Could Bear's brethren possibly get together and chip in to a large fund to get them through the day? Given the tight time frame and the fear and anxiety sweeping the street, it seemed unlikely. Firms were more focused than ever on their own self-preservation, and it would be hard to broker a group donation in the scant minutes that remained before markets began stirring.

At 6:00 A.M., the phones started beeping as a broader circle of officials joined the call. Erik Sirri and Bob Colby, his deputy in the SEC's division of trading and markets, dialed in, but their boss, Chairman Christopher Cox, did not. His deputies, not realizing the call had started so early, had not had time to notify him before joining the call themselves.

The Fed officials explained their thinking: That by providing Bear with a financial cushion to get them through Friday, they were doing their best to protect the U.S. markets from financial catastrophe. By lending money to Bear through Morgan, the central bank also was taking an unprecedented step to backstop the troubled firm, dusting off clauses in the Federal Reserve Act that hadn't been used since the 1930s. For the first time in three-quarters of a century, the government was lending money—almost directly—to an investment bank, a breed of financial institution that had long been left to sort out its own troubles.

Moreover, the Fed's loan would be nonrecourse, meaning that while it was secured by collateral assets from Bear, the government was not protected against a decline in the value of those assets. In other words, if Bear could not repay the Fed, the Fed could seize the assets—primarily bonds—that backed up the loan. But if those assets could not be sold for an amount equivalent to what the Fed had loaned Bear, the Fed would lose some of its money.

The officials' main hope was to get Bear through Friday's trading day and into the weekend, when it could work with investors toward a possible sale or other solution without the pressures of further hedge fund departures or new demands from creditors. If only they could buy that time, the officials felt, the risks to the system could be mitigated.

The call went on for another hour, as the group discussed the implications. A little after 7:00, Bernanke was interrupted by some-one from his personal security detail, wondering why he hadn't emerged from the house for a planned 7:30 breakfast with Paulson. The two got together almost every Friday morning, either at the Fed's offices or the Treasury building, next door to the White House. "I'm on the phone with him now," Bernanke replied. "I don't think we're going to make it."

Finally, Geithner laid down the gauntlet. "We've got to make a call here, because markets open at seven-thirty," he said.[*] "What's it going to be?"

The consensus was there. "Let's do it," Bernanke said.[†]

7:00 A.M.

Tim Greene had arrived at his seventh-floor trading desk at about 6:30. Most of his nineteen-person team in fixed-income funding was already there, worrying about how they were going to put together the $14 billion Bear needed that day.

Shortly after he walked in, Greene was pulled aside by Rod Mur-ray, the former mortgage salesman who handled most of the team's relationships with lenders. He led Greene into Friedman's office,

---

*Although the New York Stock Exchange and NASDAQ markets don't open for official trading until 9:30 A.M. Eastern time, the tri-party repo market and other fixed-income markets open as early as 7:30.

†In testimony given to the Senate Banking Committee on April 3, 2008, Geith-ner, who spoke on behalf of the Fed that day, summed up the central bank's thinking that morning as follows: "This action was designed to allow us to get to the weekend, and to enable us to pursue work along two tracks: first, for Bear to continue to ex-plore options with other financial institutions that might enable it to avoid bank-ruptcy; and second, for policy makers to continue the work begun on Thursday night to try to contain the risk to financial markets in the event no private-sector solution proved possible."

which was next to their desks. "I want to speak to you about something," Murray said. "I have a problem [with] going to the customer base today and asking them to lend to us over the weekend." Given how dicey Bear's position appeared to be, Murray asked, was it really ethical to accept the new money?

"It's a very valid point," said Greene. "We won't do anything till we find out what transpired overnight." Since the repo market wouldn't become active until 7:30 or so, he knew they had some time.

A few minutes later, a tired Friedman walked over to the trading desk, flashing a thumbs-up. "We're alive," he told them. "There's going to be an announcement later on," he added, describing the press release that J.P. Morgan was sending out soon.

By then Greene's other close colleagues had wandered in. Listening to Friedman talk, they stared at their boss blankly. The news didn't strike them as good. What impression would it give their lenders and counterparties that Bear had had to beg the Federal Reserve for cash?

Greene agreed. "This is horrible," he said. To him, the game was already over. Knowing what had happened, he argued, "nobody is going to lend to us." We're on life support, he thought.

Friedman was irritated. He'd been there all night, watching Bear flirt with certain death; snug in their beds at home, these guys didn't realize what had almost befallen them. He walked them through what had happened during the past twelve hours, hoping to show them how positive the lending facility really was. "You'll see," he said. The Fed money would reassure the market. But even as he spoke, he was beginning to have doubts. The repo guys usually had pretty good instincts.

From his upstairs study, Hank Paulson called the president, who was en route to New York to deliver a speech that Paulson had helped prepare on the economy.

Paulson explained the situation and the Fed's decision to provide temporary relief. He again raised concerns about the no-bailout warning.

"You've got to take that line out about the bailouts," Paulson told Bush, "because we're about to do one."

Bush took the news calmly. How bad was this Bear problem, he wanted to know, and what might it mean for the government? He asked for more details on the plans for that day.

Paulson, who was totally keyed up, was impressed by his boss's composure during such a serious crisis. He told Bush he was in luck: Bob Steel happened to be in the New York area, and would meet Bush's plane when it landed. As they traveled to the hotel where the speech was to be given, Steel could answer any questions Bush had about the crisis before the president was subjected to a grilling by the members of the day's panel and the audience. In addition to the speech, Bush was meeting a group of senior people from the *Wall Street Journal*, including Rupert Murdoch, the paper's owner.

Paulson was nothing if not blunt. At Goldman, where he'd spent most of his career, colleagues had joked that he suffered from "brain-to-mouth" disease, saying whatever popped into his head, regardless of the consequences. Perhaps realizing his uncensored manner, he preferred the telephone to e-mail and was famous for dispatching voice mails to colleagues at all hours of the day and weekend. If intrigued by a topic, he could talk for hours. If not, he could summarily end a conversation.

His background was unusual for Wall Street. Raised in the farm town of Barrington, on the outskirts of Chicago, Paulson came from a strict family of Christian Scientists. He didn't drink alcohol and liked to go to bed early, sometimes leaving work functions as early as 8:45 P.M. He'd been married to his wife, Wendy, for more than thirty years, and as the head of Goldman's Chicago office in the 1980s and early 1990s, he'd commuted more than an hour a day from Barrington, sticking to the simple way of life he'd grown up with—albeit on a sprawling piece of property.

Unlike many Wall Street couples who spent time on the tennis court or golf green, the Paulsons got a kick out of watching birds. Starting in 1994, when Hank's job had moved them to New York, Wendy began organizing an early-morning bird-watching trip with friends in Central Park, near their Upper West Side apartment. Many exotic species flew through the park on their journeys to points north or south, and it was a place to make some great finds. Birds would fly over the concrete jungle for a while, alighting the moment they spotted that oasis of green. Hank loved the early-morning ritual and during the warbler season in April and May would often join her for half an hour on his way to Goldman around 6:00 A.M., his car and driver idling on a side street. Then he'd continue downtown to the firm's headquarters on 85 Broad Street.

The Paulsons donated money to numerous environmental causes, reserving special assistance for the Nature Conservancy—where he was a board member—and the Peregrine Fund, a nonprofit that conserves endangered birds of prey. In recognition of his generosity (and to solicit new donations), the group sent a falconer every year to Goldman's offices with an exotic bird of prey. Sitting around a conference room, Paulson's staff would watch in awe as the bird eyed them nastily, fluttered its wings, and defecated on the table. They were leery, but the boss was delighted.

Paulson, a former football player of rigid bearing, was feared and respected around the firm. Even in the carnivorous culture of Goldman, he stood out. He had ousted his cochief executive, Jon Corzine, during the man's Christmas vacation in 1998, and emerged as the sole CEO. During the interim period between the holidays and Corzine's official departure, the humiliation of Paulson's political coup was so great that Corzine hid in his town car outside the Goldman offices, and had his secretary bring documents downstairs and slip them through the window.

During the spring of 1999, Paulson led the firm through a wildly successful initial public offering, largely on the back of Corzine, who had done much of the spade work to convince investors and employees that the deal was a good idea. In the years that followed, Corzine pursued a political career, eventually becoming senator and later governor of New Jersey, as Paulson steered Goldman through an unprecedented period of growth and profits. In 2006, after being tapped to lead the Treasury during the waning years of Bush's second term, Paulson anointed Lloyd Blankfein, a brash, whip-smart former gold salesman, to run Goldman. Soon after, the Paulsons packed up their Upper West Side home and decamped to Washington, D.C., where they planned to start a new life.

But Paulson couldn't forget his investment banking roots. And on this Friday morning, he was in full-on deal mode. Pacing his second-story home office, he was so distracted by phone calls—with Geithner, with Bush, and with his own people—that he couldn't find the time to step into a shower. He was running on adrenaline, hoping the government's quickie agreement to float Bear would stave off any major market losses or additional bank failures until the company could sell itself to another entity.

But he was also angry. How could Bear's executives have let themselves get to such a precarious point—overnight? It was something out of his worst nightmares. In the wee hours of that morning, unable to toss and turn any longer, he'd switched on the television to see whether bad news was coming out of Asian trading yet. The headlines from overseas had seemed unaffected by the life-or-death drama at Bear, about which no new details had been disclosed. Still, it was the sort of paranoia that Paulson could do without.

As Goldman's CEO, Paulson had always planned for financial Armageddon. The firm had simply had too many brushes with death. In 1994, five years before its initial public offering, a slew of trading losses led the firm to a painful round of layoffs and political infighting. Since it was not yet a public company, Goldman was operating on partner capital at the time, and its most senior executives were seeing their own money almost wiped out. Dozens of partners left, including the company's head partner, Stephen Friedman, who quit abruptly, forcing Paulson, who had been named vice chairman, to relocate from Barrington to New York practically overnight to help stabilize the company.

After the firm went public, he decided to grow its cash reserves. Goldman had for years kept a stash of bonds in a lockbox managed by the Bank of New York that was never invested, even in low-risk securities. It was the firm's rainy-day fund. If ever Goldman's lenders refused to extend credit, it could dip into the stash directly, without worrying about liquidating its holdings in securities or waiting for a counterparty to cough up the money.

Over the years, Paulson became notorious for wanting to hoard additional securities in the lockbox. Whenever trading conditions appeared to be bad, he would approach Goldman's chief financial officer, David Viniar, and ask him to add to the pile. "Put some more securities in the BONY box," Paulson would say. Viniar, a fellow cynic, understood the need for liquidity. You could never be too careful, he knew.

As Goldman's business grew during the technology boom and a new emphasis on proprietary trading generated fat returns, a run on the bank seemed less and less likely. But Paulson continued growing the cash reserves. By the time he resigned in 2006 to become Treasury secretary, the sum had grown to some $60 billion. These days, under Blankfein, it was heading toward $100 billion.

Now, focusing on the tumultuous day ahead, Paulson called Geithner. As he thought through the problems with Bear's model, something new was bothering him: Alan Schwartz. The CEO struck him as a deer in the headlights.

"I wonder if Alan Schwartz really understands what in essence he's done," Paulson told the New York Fed president. Bear had been desperate for cash, he said, so Schwartz had grabbed a lifeline. But did the Bear CEO really understand that he had lost his autonomy in the process? "The government's on the line," Paulson said. "He's essentially in the hands of the government." In other words, whatever the Fed and the Treasury thought was best for the country was what they'd expect Schwartz to do.

Geithner looked at it the same way. He had talked one-on-one that morning to Schwartz, in the hopes of making the same point: The Fed doesn't just hand over billions of dollars with no strings attached. "I tried to explain that," Geithner told Paulson. "But why don't you call him. You're good at these things."

Schwartz was in a meeting when Paulson's call came in. He seemed nervous. Paulson tried to explain his view. "You're going to file for bankruptcy, and then the Federal Reserve comes in and has to extend credit," he told the CEO. "You realize you're not operating in a normal environment."

Schwartz said he understood. He was relieved, in fact, to hear what Paulson had called to say. "I thought you were going to deliver a different message," he replied.

But you are no longer in charge, Paulson thought. He wasn't sure the idea was coming across. "Maybe this is an inelegant way to put it," he told Schwartz, "but you are in the hands of the government."

"Tim told me much the same thing," Schwartz said.

8:30 A.M.

On the sixth floor, it was chaos. The elation people had felt at hearing about the Fed assist soon gave way to a panicked obsession over the language of the press release. Naturally, Bear wanted the wording to sound as upbeat as possible, as though they'd be carrying on business as usual. They also wanted to hint that, just in case things didn't go well, J.P. Morgan was keen to buy them. But there was debate over how explicit to be about Bear's talks with other parties.

Another flashpoint was the length of time the Fed money would last. The Fed and J.P. Morgan had proposed suggesting twenty-eight days, a figure that would take Bear well beyond the critical day ahead and give the public the idea that Bear was safe for the moment. Bear lawyers, however, wanted maximum flexibility. They wanted to say "at least twenty-eight days," in order to leave their options open. But the other side held firm. It would be twenty-eight days at the most, Bear was told.

During these debates, Upton scurried between Bear general counsel Michael Solender, Molinaro, Schwartz, and Metrick, all of who were offering opinions on the text. He'd reach a consensus of his executives, then e-mail a suggested change to J.P. Morgan, dashing up and down the hallway from Solender's office on one corner of the floor to Molinaro's on the other, stopping at his own computer in between to key in changes. But after ninety minutes going back and forth, Upton snapped. "We gotta get this thing done!" he told Metrick. "Get it into the marketplace."

But the executives couldn't figure out which version was the final copy. Upton made a quick round of checks, grabbed a printout of what he thought was the right draft, and was rushing over to a copier when Metrick came screaming out of Molinaro's office, where Schwartz and the CFO were waiting. "Give me the fucking document already!" Metrick bellowed at Upton. "I'm trying to get it fucking finished!" Upton screamed back. He hurtled toward the copier, draft in hand.

Some fifteen minutes later, at 9:13, J.P. Morgan's official press release went out on the business wire and was blasted all over computer news feeds and on CNBC. "JP Morgan Chase and Federal Reserve Board of New York to Provide Financing to Bear Stearns," it read. The release went on to say that the bank and the government would together lend Bear "secured funding," or money backed by collateral, for "an initial period of up to 28 days." Its last sentence was the most intriguing: "JPMorgan Chase is working closely with Bear Stearns on securing permanent financing or other alternatives for the company."

Then, at 9:21, a similarly worded release from Bear was issued. This one contained a disclaimer from Schwartz. "Our liquidity position in the last 24 hours had significantly deteriorated," the CEO stated. "We took this important step to restore confidence in us in the marketplace, strengthen our liquidity and allow us to continue normal operations." Neither press release contained a statement of support from the Fed, whose full board had not yet met to officially approve the nonrecourse loan.

In the seventeen minutes between the issuance of the first release and the opening of U.S. stock markets for official trading, Bear shares launched an impressive rally, rising more than 9 percent, to more than $62 per share. Mortgage traders on the seventh floor were thrilled. As Friedman strode through the bond-sales department outside his office, he got a standing ovation. "We're alive!" somebody yelled. The cost of purchasing insurance protection against a default by Bear on its debts was dropping to its lowest point in days, and there was gleeful talk about how the so-called "shorts"—traders hoping to make money on Bear shares' decline—would get "squeezed," or lose their shirts. Employees high-fived one another, believing the worst was over.

Steve Black was packing his things in Anguilla when he caught word of the stock activity on CNBC. J.P. Morgan had located a corporate jet in Miami, and it was on its way to whisk the executive and his family back to New York. He shook his head. "People don't understand what just happened here," he told his wife. "I guarantee by the time we land, that stock is going to be in half."

A few minutes later, the New York Stock Exchange opened for business, and those purchasing Bear shares during the light before-market trading period were replaced by a gusher of sellers. The stock quickly erased its gains and began a swift drop.

Down in Washington, Paulson was hosting a conference call with industry executives. He was nervous about their reaction to the bailout. These were unprecedented moves, and there was no way of knowing whether the firms would behave in good conscience or prey on a troubled competitor.

On his way to work that morning, he had toyed with the right language to use on the call. Sitting in the backseat of the car, he sketched out some phrases on a legal pad. He didn't want to sound too punitive. He decided to put it to the firms straight, but with a polite tone: I expect you to behave yourselves. With any luck, the Bear crisis would bring out the more gentlemanly side of Wall Street that had prevailed during the Long-Term meltdown.

The call began ominously. Technical difficulties made it hard to hear some people. Schwartz was dialing in from a patchy cell phone, and Dimon didn't surface until the conversation was fifteen or twenty minutes under way. Fuld, Thain, and John Mack, the CEO of Morgan Stanley, waited patiently. Goldman copresident Gary Cohn wondered why it was so chaotic.

When things finally settled down, Paulson was the first to speak. "I want you to deal with Bear Stearns as a responsible counterparty," he told the group. "When you're at a company, you think about protecting yourself at all times," he added. But these were not normal times. He expected firms not to make unreasonable collateral demands, and to trade in good faith with the troubled firm.

Schwartz and Dimon, who by now was finally connected, made some brief remarks, not saying much beyond what was already contained in the press releases.

There was a flurry of questions, most of which sought greater clarity on the meaning of the Fed facility. How much risk would the government be taking on? some wondered. With the central bank using government money to backstop a troubled investment bank, they were suddenly wandering around in virgin territory. Little new information, however, was given. Everyone was waiting to see how the day would play out.

Meanwhile, in the nation's stock markets, Bear wasn't the only one hurting. Within the first hour of trading, the Dow Jones Industrial Average, the index that tracks blue chip stocks, had fallen more than 300 points, with twenty-nine of its thirty component stocks taking losses. Other financial names, including J.P. Morgan itself, were tumbling.

Having arrived at the airport, Black found a television. He couldn't believe how fast the stock declines had been. He had expected Bear shares to fall by the time he landed in four or five hours—not forty-five minutes after the opening.

Among investors, the crisis of confidence had returned in force. "People realized that Bear Stearns just came out the other day saying everything was fine," Paul Nolte, director of investments at the small firm Hinsdale Associates, told the Dow Jones Newswires. "So, two days later, why would they need this funding from the Fed and J.P. Morgan? If it's like that for them, what is it like for Merrill Lynch or for Thornburg Mortgage?"

By then the Federal Reserve Board had gathered in its headquarters in the Foggy Bottom section of Washington and approved the emergency loan. Bernanke and his colleagues hated the thought of financing a bank run with government dollars, but they knew that helping Bear survive the day would be better than allowing it to collapse. The vote was unanimous.

LATER FRIDAY
March 14, 2008

10:00 A.M.

Calls were pouring in to Bear's investor-relations and financial divisions. Sequestered in his office on the sixth floor, Molinaro could hardly keep up with his phone messages. He was being slammed with questions from Bear's investors, all of who were wondering what the Fed facility meant for the stock. Some were encouraged by the initial rally that morning, but worried about the long-term impact for their holdings.

The most painful call, however, came from his daughter, Danielle. A sophomore at Boston College, his eldest had seen the news of the Fed bailout being reported on CNBC that morning, and was terrified as to what it meant for her family. Not long after the press release was issued, she called Molinaro, crying.

He tried to reassure her. "It's okay, everything's going to be okay," he said, trying not to let his frayed nerves show. "Stuff happens. It's not the end of the world." He wasn't sure if she believed him.

Bear, as Molinaro knew it, was over. The firm was in dire jeopardy, and reality was only starting to sink in. He had invested more than two decades in the place, and it was coming apart at the seams. All those hours, all those sleepless nights—for nothing.

Molinaro had seen lean times before. He grew up in the sleepy suburban town of Endwell, New York, a few miles outside of Binghamton. His father, Sam Sr., was a child of the Depression who had left school in the seventh grade to go to work. He and his wife, Josephine, had moved to Endwell from their hometown of Carbondale, Pennsylvania, to escape the economic hard times that had befallen their region.

In Binghamton, Molinaro's father took a job selling cars at the Miller Dodge dealership on Main Street. Then in his midforties,

Sam Sr. was well liked by his colleagues and clients. He was hard-working, a gentleman, and—perhaps most important in a small town like that—not conceited. Locals took pride in their community, and trust mattered.

Sam Jr. largely kept to himself. With a twelve-year age gap between him and his middle brother, Jim, he was for years the only child in the house. During high school in the Maine-Endwell public school system, less than a mile up the road from the family home, he participated in neither clubs nor athletics.

After high school Molinaro moved to western New York, where he attended St. Bonaventure University, a Catholic college, and majored in accounting. He spent the first few years after graduation working for the accounting firm Price Waterhouse in Syracuse until his future wife, Lisa Melillo, a New Yorker he had met at St. Bonaventure, convinced him to try out the big city instead. The couple married in 1983, shortly after Molinaro was transferred to the firm's Manhattan office. They started out in Queens and eventually moved to suburban Connecticut, having three children along the way.

Molinaro was hired at Bear in 1986. As he worked his way up the ladder there, his lifestyle improved markedly. In 1996, the family bought a vacation home in the Cape Cod town of Harwich, Massachusetts. As his children got older and needed less hands-on attention, Molinaro began playing more golf, primarily at the Burning Tree Country Club in Greenwich, Connecticut. He eventually whittled his handicap down to 14.

In 2003, the family bought a sweeping, gated home in New Canaan, Connecticut, for $5 million. It was a far cry from the one-story house Molinaro had grown up in in Endwell. As CFO he was making a multimillion-dollar salary. In 2006, the company's best year ever, he took home a bonus of nearly $13 million—making him the best-paid executive after Cayne, Schwartz, and Spector, each of whom received more than $16 million. Greenberg, who had by then relinquished his chairman post and ran the executive committee, took home $9 million.

Molinaro was a workaholic who arrived early in the morning and stayed late. Colleagues were as impressed with his level of commitment to the company as they were annoyed by his disorganization. He was jovial and impeccably groomed, his salt-and-pepper hair always combed back just so, his French cuffs buttoned neatly with tasteful studs. Unlike Cayne or Spector, he was eager to improve things and willing to take criticism—sometimes too willing.

Employees and coworkers were fond of him. But within the upper ranks of Bear, Molinaro was often in an awkward spot. He understood the importance of the company's image, and of being cautious with the firm's resources, yet it was hard to affect change. Meetings with Cayne could be raucous and unproductive. Schwartz was often too distracted by his own client matters to worry about general firm business. Spector was a highly competent manager, but his growing arrogance and frequent clashes with Cayne were creating tension during management meetings.

The two had long had a love-hate relationship. Cayne had introduced himself to Spector in 1987 after a routine review of year-end compensation figures. Spector, then a young trader on Bear's nascent mortgage-backed securities desk, was raking in enormous pay despite his relatively junior level. Cayne was impressed, and when he learned that as a high school student in Chevy Chase, Maryland, Spector had been named the "king of bridge"—a huge honor in the world of young competitive card players—the two became fast friends. By 1990, Spector had been named to the board. Shortly thereafter, he became head of fixed income, arguably the firm's most important operational position.

During the years that followed, Spector and Schwartz were promoted in tandem, but with his knowledge of the firm's core business, Spector was always considered the more likely candidate for CEO. By

2001, he was running Bear's entire sales and trading divisions in both stocks and bonds, as well as the firm's asset-management unit. Schwartz was responsible only for investment banking. Private-client services, the personal brokerage unit, was overseen largely by Cayne himself.

Cayne appeared to feel threatened by Spector's growing prominence. As he faced his seventieth birthday, he showed no interest in retirement, telling people privately that he'd be the last CEO of Bear. Spector, once an occasional dinner guest of Cayne and his wife, was no longer invited over.

During the presidential campaign of 2004, Spector, an ardent Democrat, spoke out on behalf of Senator John Kerry. The sitting Bush administration, he said at a press conference, "[has displayed] very short-term, narrow-minded policies." Cayne, a Republican, was furious. No Bear executive should publicly endorse a candidate, he felt. It was an embarrassment for the firm to show its hand that way.

Cayne demanded that Spector issue an apology to the firm's employees, but Spector refused. So a few weeks later, Cayne made one himself. "If any of you were upset or offended by these press reports, please accept both his and my apologies," he wrote in an internal e-mail, referring to Spector. Individual Bear executives, Cayne added, were to refrain "in any circumstance" from publicly expressing political views without the consent of management. Molinaro stood by and watched as the embarrassing imbroglio went public.

Months later, the CFO was reviewing some compensation estimates when he made a troubling realization: Spector was accumulating hundreds of millions of dollars in long-term pay, draining Bear's capital at an alarming rate.

The trouble was, Spector was entirely within his rights. Under a capital accumulation plan, or CAP, that had been enacted years earlier, top Bear executives were entitled to defer 100 percent of their income until retirement. The deferred pay was held in units that were convertible into stock, and those units paid an annual dividend far higher than a typical stock dividend. As the total sum grew larger, the payouts from Bear's coffers rose, too.

Spector's deferred pay loomed large already, and Molinaro knew it could grow far bigger. He shivered at the thought. Not only was it shortsighted financial planning, it was terrible for Bear's public image. Just the prior year, Dick Grasso had been run out of his job as chairman and CEO of the New York Stock Exchange for receiving what some deemed to be overly high pay of nearly $187.5 million, a comparable amount. Board members—a panel of Wall Street and outside directors that included Hank Paulson and Cayne himself— had approved the payouts, but when the actual numbers leaked out, the public had been outraged. It was simply too much, people thought, for one man running a not-for-profit company. A brewing front-running scandal involving traders who bought and sold shares on the exchange floor only worsened perceptions. Institutional investors excoriated Grasso, who had served the NYSE for nearly forty years, and Attorney General Eliot Spitzer ultimately launched an investigation into whether the pay was improper. In 2004, Spitzer sued Grasso, asserting that the pay was improper for a not-for-profit chief. In July 2008, however, a technical victory allowed Grasso to prevail, enabling him to keep the money he had already received. Spitzer's successor as attorney general, Andrew Cuomo, declined to pursue the case further.

In 2004, Molinaro approached Spector privately. "You could be the CEO when this thing blows up on you," he told the copresident. "It's too good. You've gotta get rid of it." Spector refused.

Reluctantly, Molinaro took the matter to Cayne. He couldn't talk sense into Spector, he explained, and something had to be done. Cayne agreed, and demanded that Spector cash out.

Spector was irate. He had the money coming to him, and he couldn't believe Cayne was bigfooting him like this. He complained to board members, telling them Cayne's orders were unreasonable.

But Cayne won the argument. Spector agreed to take his roughly $200 million distribution, and CAP was modified to avoid future problems—with the loophole that had led to Spector's big payout permanently shelved.

Except for the Kerry flap, which had made the *Wall Street Journal*'s "Bids & Offers" column, Bear managed to keep most of these run-ins under wraps. Its press office was notoriously guarded, often evading reporter phone calls. When the press did hear snippets of Bear's internal politics, the communications officers would often claim, convincingly, that they knew nothing of the subject at hand. Meanwhile, Bear's executives lay low in public.

Most managers at Bear thought the system made perfect sense. They quietly kept to themselves, preserving the firm's clubby mystique. Bear was like a place where you could get rich if you found a profitable niche for yourself—a culture often described as "eat what you kill." It was the opposite of a place like Goldman, which was a far more "franchise"-driven culture, where the brand name superseded individuals in importance. And Bear employees liked it that way.

Bear's insular mentality was emphasized to new hires. In an annual lecture to the fixed-income division's summer interns, for instance, Paul Friedman liked to talk about something he referred to as "C-1 risk." Unlike market risk or credit risk, which addressed scenarios in which Bear's capital was threatened by gyrations in the environment or the health of its counterparties, C-1 risk referred to the money that could be lost by news articles written about the firm in the "Money & Investing" section of the *Wall Street Journal*. Mentions of Wall Street firms in that section were rarely flattering, Friedman felt, and investors were prone to sell stock when they saw it covered there. He was proud to tell the interns that Bear rarely was.

Bear's secrecy, however, became a liability when it came to courting the financial analysts who gave investors advice on whether to buy stock in the company. This was a longstanding source of frustration to Molinaro. He and his investor-relations staff had struggled over the years to win the analyst coverage they felt Bear deserved.

Despite its booming bond sales and trading business, which had benefited immensely from the surge in new mortgages and the trading of related securities, Bear's successes in other areas were limited. Its prime-brokerage unit, one of the oldest and largest on the Street, was strong, and the investment-banking clients in Schwartz's division were loyal. But Bear's presence in Europe and Asia, where firms like Goldman Sachs had expanded rapidly in the 1990s and 2000s, was extremely weak, and its internal money manager, Bear Stearns Asset Management, was by far the smallest on Wall Street. Before the hedge fund blowups of 2007, BSAM had just $60 billion under management—far less than its closest competitor, Lehman Brothers, which had $263 billion.

Molinaro and his team knew their firm's business wasn't broad enough. Nonetheless, they felt they had a good story to tell, and blamed their executive team for not getting it out. The number-one problem was Cayne. Blunt to a fault, he could not be counted on to position Bear attractively for analysts. In public settings, his interactions with them were too short to leave much impression. What he did say was sometimes memorable for the wrong reasons.

Goldman Sachs brokerage firm analyst Bill Tanona had once arrived three or four minutes late to a Bear analyst gathering held in the firm's auditorium. Seeing that Cayne was first on the schedule but not the executive on the stage, Tanona sidled up to a hedge fund analyst he knew and asked why the CEO wasn't speaking. "He already did," the analyst replied. Tanona was shocked.

During a question-and-answer session with Cayne on another Bear investment day when the firm's stock was flying high, one of the brokerage-firm analysts asked innocently if Cayne planned to have the company buy back any stock—a common tactic for returning capital to shareholders, reducing the number of shares outstanding, and boosting the earnings per share.

"Why would I buy the stock when it trades at well over book value?" Cayne replied, indicating that the stock was far above the price he'd want to pay for it.

Some of the analysts looked stunned. Watching from the sidelines, Molinaro was mortified. You want these people to recommend the stock to their clients, he thought, and yet you think it's too expensive. Afterward, he scrambled to backtrack, telling attendees that Cayne had spoken out of context.

Over time, Molinaro and Elizabeth Ventura, the firm's investor-relations chief, tried to set up more intimate gatherings where Cayne could showcase his infamous charm while remaining comfortably plainspoken. In some cases, it worked. Relaxed and able to talk candidly with the Bear CEO about business matters over a few drinks, Cayne was surprisingly likable at the small dinners. There, even when he said things his team wished he wouldn't—like his comment in the spring of 2007 that his biggest concern was the firm's wavering stock price at a time when the mortgage market had begun to crater—they could rest assured knowing that Cayne's comments had been off the record and were unlikely to pop up later on in research reports.

With such truculent superiors, Molinaro was often forced to deal with the investing public himself. But of course, he couldn't keep up with all the phone calls, leaving the impression that, again, Bear was behind the ball. Analysts were rarely granted one-on-one meetings with management, so they didn't have much insight into Bear's strategies or results. Reporters remained baffled by the company, and when they needed something to write, they fell back on the same old chestnuts about Cayne's bridge games and the sarcastic memos that former head partner Alan "Ace" Greenberg had sent out in the 1980s. Molinaro bristled at Bear's image, but could do little to combat it.

His close colleagues, who dealt with Bear's financing, often wondered why he didn't stand up to his superiors. For years, the firm had been overreliant on short-term financing like commercial paper, and an ongoing debate raged between equity traders and the treasurer's office over whether Bear's handling of client cash would raise problems during a time of crisis. Through it all, Molinaro seemed unable to play the heavy, holding discussions over and over again without coming down on either side.

Now, on March 14, facing his most hectic morning ever, Molinaro spoke to a frantic financial-sector analyst at Neuberger Berman, the large institutional investor owned by Lehman Brothers.

A bit earlier, at 10:25 A.M. the Fed had issued its own brief press release, noting that it was "monitoring market developments closely" and that it would "continue to provide liquidity as necessary to promote the orderly functioning of the financial system." It added that the board had voted unanimously on the Bear bailout that morning.

But the Neuberger analyst, confused by the morning's news, was imploring Molinaro to issue a better explanation of what the Fed facility meant for Bear, in hopes of curbing the massive downswing that was by then under way. "This is not a bad thing, it's a good thing," the analyst told Molinaro. "Why is the market treating it like it's a bad thing?"

Molinaro realized he was right. If Bear wanted to reassure investors, it needed to speak more freely about its position. Granted, the company was still under tremendous pressure, but it had just won a lifeline, he reasoned: twenty-eight days in which to do a deal or come up with another solution.

Molinaro called Dennis Block, who had just returned to Cadwalader's downtown offices after camping out at 383 all night. The drive to his home on Long Island was too long, so he had skipped it altogether. Molinaro wondered how the language of the press release should be interpreted, he told Block; he was being showered with questions about safety and soundness. Assure the market that you're okay, the lawyer told him. That was the message that needed to get out.

Molinaro called Schwartz. What did the CEO think about holding a conference call with investors? Schwartz agreed that it was a good idea. Molinaro talked to his investor-relations chief, who began setting up a call for midday.

Molinaro needed a break. He knew he couldn't face any more angry and frightened investors—let alone the media—without a shower and some fresh air. He took the elevator downstairs to the lobby.

It was a crisp, lovely day in midtown Manhattan. Walking up Madison, he passed dozens of people on their way to work, who were no doubt blissfully unaware of the life-and-death battle being waged at number 383. If only he could freshen up with some new clothes, he thought, maybe he could put on a game face and pass for one of those people.

After a few minutes of walking, he couldn't find an open men's shop, so he settled for an iced coffee from Starbucks. Then he went to the Bear gym, took a quick shower, and put the same clothes back on.

Around 10:15, Paul Friedman heard from a trader friend at Barclays via e-mail. "How you holding up?" asked the friend.

"I was here all night working on this JPM thing," replied Friedman. "Running on fumes right now. Didn't expect this horrible reaction."

"Perception is JP is going to cherry-pick a few divisions, and let the rest of BSC"—the stock-ticker abbreviation for Bear Stearns Companies—"go under," the Barclay's trader added. "It seems to be wrong, but the [market] is killing it."

"Killing it is an understatement."

"Why JP? Seems to me they are tapping the window for you," wrote the trader, referring to the Federal Reserve "window," at which banks borrowed when they had no other lenders available.

"Had no time. Needed someone in New York with lots of money and without their own problems. Pretty much ruled out Citi. Also,

JPM had the most exposure to us and the most to lose. Didn't expect them to strong-arm the Fed into taking the risk and making it a bailout."

"Someone has to stabilize the stock now or it will be irrelevant."

"Agreed," wrote Friedman. "Didn't expect this insane response to it but I guess I should have. But when they write the book on this one I can say 'I was there.'"

During this exchange, Friedman was getting worrisome signals from his counterparts around the firm. Fidelity Investments, the large Boston mutual-fund company, was raising a stink about two trades it had done with Bear: a $7 billion repo loan it had made early that morning, and a $1 billion mortgage loan they had arranged sometime ago. Given that they hadn't known until midmorning about Bear's deteriorating position, Fidelity now wanted out of both.

Late that morning, Upton went up to the seventh floor to confer with Friedman and Mayer. To him, the decision was simple: Let Fidelity out of the $7 billion repo loan—which was collateralized by U.S. Treasury bonds that would be good with other lenders—but hold firm on the smaller transaction. After all, it had been in the works before that morning, and had a one-month maturity date that didn't fall until April.

Mayer thought the solution seemed reasonable, so Upton walked Friedman back to his office, where they called Fidelity. The Boston traders immediately launched into a diatribe about how Bear had dealt with their company in poor faith, and that holding Fidelity's feet to the fire wasn't fair. "What's fair is that you guys got into a Treasury trade this morning that you thought was inappropriate, so we're going to let you out of that," Upton told them. But the mortgage trade, he said, "has been on the books for a while, is not an overnight trade that you did today, and we're not going to break it." But Fidelity really wanted out, the traders said. "Be fucking grateful that we let you out of the Treasury trade," snapped Upton, hanging up.

He was far more concerned about the rating agencies, which were now threatening to downgrade Bear on the news from that morning. Those decisions, while expected, could wreak havoc on the company by stoking doubts that it would make good on its debt. If lenders had further concerns about Bear's ability to pay them back, that could make it even more difficult for the firm to raise short-term funding.

Upton knew the importance of managing rating-agency relationships. But in this case, he had been deprived of his usual opportunity to warn them about the pending news. Things had simply unfolded too fast.

He called Standard & Poor's, Moody's, Fitch, and the large Canadian agency DBRS from his office, making his best attempt at damage control. "You saw the announcement this morning," he told them. "We had significant deterioration in our liquidity the last couple of days." He stressed that he still felt the Fed facility was a positive, as it ensured secured funding for up to a month.

Upton knew not to expect too much. He assured the agencies he expected nothing short of a downgrade. But if there were any questions he could answer to help them better understand the terms of the Fed loan, he said, he was there for them. After that, all he could do was wait to see just how dubious they were.

He turned to his messages from Bear's investors. PIMCO, T. Rowe Price, and Dreyfus had called. He began dialing them back.

Meanwhile, in the prime-brokerage department, the mass exodus was continuing. Fed facility or no, hedge funds still felt unsafe keeping their balances with Bear, and the firm was again losing billions of dollars at once.

Bear was grappling with an old-fashioned run on the bank. But instead of having long lines of individuals waiting to cancel accounts that had thousands of dollars of deposits, the firm had large-scale institutions yanking hundreds of millions—in some cases billions—at a time. The public had simply lost faith in Bear. During the week, as the stock price struggled and the rumors persisted, rival firms, mutual funds, hedge funds, and other sophisticated players had had their doubts. But now that the Fed was giving Bear nonrecourse loan money to keep it afloat, there was no question in people's minds that the firm was all but lost, and these institutions didn't want their money to go down with it.

On Tim Greene's desk, confusion now reigned. He and his team had heroically managed to raise nearly the entire $14 billion in new money. But now they were in talks with their counterparts at J.P. Morgan, who were driving a hard bargain. The firm's lenders and lawyers were unsure how to interpret the language in the press release, so they wanted to play it very safe. They wanted only AAA, or "triple-A," collateral, meaning the very safest bonds and other securities, and they were asking for large "haircuts" on every loan—meaning that for every dollar J.P. Morgan provided, it wanted as much as $.20 in cash. But Bear didn't have that sort of cash lying around.

Across the floor in his own office, Tom Marano was also being barraged with phone calls and e-mails. He tried to strike an upbeat tone as friends wrote to say they were praying for him and for Bear. "Don't count us out," he told some. "Still swinging," he said to others.

He was concerned about what he viewed as predatory behavior on the part of Bear's trading counterparts. Earlier in the week, he believed that the major Wall Street firms had backed off trading with Bear over worries that the company would collapse and not make good on its debts. Ironically, the media attention that had begun with Schwartz's ill-fated CNBC interview on Wednesday morning appeared to have had the positive effect of shaming those firms into trading with Bear again.

But new rumors abounded. One of Marano's mortgage salesmen had sent a worrisome e-mail around, saying that his contacts at the

Royal Bank of Canada had told him that the firm "might have issues" with Bear as a counterparty. The salesman was asking for
Schwartz or Molinaro to call a senior official at RBC and have it out
with him. "This is a real problem," he had written.[*]

Around lunchtime, Marano got a call from one of the players he
suspected was shorting the stock: Ken Griffin, the chief executive of
the Chicago-based hedge fund company Citadel. He and Griffin had
been exchanging calls and e-mails about another matter that week,
and now the CEO was ostensibly calling to see if he could help Marano's ailing firm.

"Is there anything I can do?" Griffin asked. He had had a similar
conversation with Schwartz the prior morning that had come to
nothing.

Marano had heard too many rumors about Citadel shorting Bear
stock to take Griffin very seriously. He had enough on his plate that
day. "There's such concern that you're short that I wouldn't even go
there," he said.

"I'm not short," Griffin said. If Bear executives doubted what he
said, they were welcome to come to Chicago and review Citadel's
trading positions, he added.

Griffin was frustrated. He saw a compelling opportunity in Bear
and was eager for an invitation to come take a look. His company
wasn't just a hedge fund, though many of Citadel's competitors regarded it as such. Over the past year or so, Citadel had established a
team of people who specialized in vetting distressed companies with
an eye toward making good, cheap investments. The previous summer, Citadel had bought the troubled hedge fund Sowood Capital,
and a few months ago, the struggling brokerage E*TRADE. Now
both Schwartz and Marano were brushing him off.

---

[*]A spokeswoman for RBC denies that the bank backed away from Bear, saying
that, in fact, RBC increased the amount of short-term funding it made available to
the firm through the March crisis.

11:45 A.M.

Rodge Cohen, the banking expert and chairman of the prestigious downtown Manhattan law firm Sullivan & Cromwell, was running to catch a noon flight home from Washington, D.C., when his cell phone rang. It was Tese and Salerno, calling from Florida.

"We've got some real issues to deal with," the directors told Cohen as he paced the US Airways wing of Reagan National Airport.

"I know," said Cohen, a slight, impeccably groomed securities-law wonk. He had spent the morning meeting with officials from the Fed and the Treasury on behalf of another client, and the officials couldn't help being distracted by the Bear news. They gave Cohen the strong impression that the government was unlikely to provide much further assistance.

For months now, Cohen had been consulting with Schwartz on ways to help Bear navigate the credit crisis. He had good contacts at the Fed and was more intimately acquainted with banking and central bank matters—especially as they pertained to investment banks—than almost anyone. Since the prior fall, he had been advocating on behalf of Bear and other firms for the Fed to consider opening the discount window, hoping that if a cash crunch were ever to come, the firm could count on the government's largess, just like any commercial bank. But officials had steadfastly resisted.

Now Tese and Salerno wanted to know if Cohen could represent them and Bear's other independent directors.

"I've been working with Alan," Cohen replied. "I assume he's okay with this?"

They said Schwartz had consented.

That left only the possibility of conflicts with other clients represented by Sullivan & Cromwell, a standard question lawyers would ask before taking on any new business. "Let me make sure I can do this," said Cohen, "and I'll get back to you."

12:30 P.M.

Promptly at 12:30, thousands of analysts and investors convened for the Bear conference call. Molinaro made brief opening remarks, announcing that the firm's first-quarter earnings report had been moved up from later the following week to Monday. Then Schwartz took over.

Bear, he said, had been subjected to a great deal of "rumor and innuendo" in the past week. As a result, he explained, our "liquidity situation deteriorated." Demands from customers, lenders, and counterparties had strained Bear's resources to a point where it had been forced to look at "alternatives." Bankers at Lazard, he added, were helping at that very moment to sort those through. He offered no guidance as to how soon the company might be sold.

Indeed, Gary Parr had spent the morning on the phone at 383, canvasing more potential investors. J.P. Morgan had people in the building, and Flowers had arrived with its own team of analysts. But he needed to cast the net wider. Bear was interested in a significant investment, an acquisition, or possibly even a rapid sale of the prime-brokerage business—anything to restore market confidence and create some more liquidity to work with.

Parr had spoken to the CEO of the Bank of New York Mellon and a senior official in Deutsche Bank's U.S. operations. BONY seemed uninterested, but Deutsche Bank appeared to be a possibility. He knew it would depend on what the big bosses in Germany thought.

Schwartz opened the call to questions. Guy Moszkowski, a Merrill Lynch analyst, was one of the first to speak up. He had a "buy" rating on the company and a price target of close to $100 and wanted to know if Bear's "book value," the self-determined value of its assets—then estimated at a little more than $80 per share—still held. Molinaro said it did.

There was a question about the pace at which prime-brokerage clients were withdrawing money from the firm: Had the pace accelerated that day?

Molinaro stumbled. "It has been, I think, more or less—I don't want to say at a higher level or a lower level—not materially different from what we've been dealing with during the week on that side." His answer didn't make a lot of sense.

There were a couple of questions about the time frame associated with the Fed loans: How long would the loans last, and what was the purpose of them? Glenn Schorr, a UBS AG securities analyst, asked.

Schwartz avoided the timing question. The key, he said, was to continue conducting business as usual. He viewed the loan as "a bridge [to] a more permanent solution." That solution could be anything that allowed Bear to work with customers and to maximize shareholder value, he added.

There were no more questions after that.

2:00 P.M.

It had been a brutal week for David Kim, who worked in Bear's legal department handling documents related to derivatives trades. The Moody's downgrade on Monday had triggered the possibility that dozens of Bear's counterparties would back away. Kim and his colleagues spent the week scrambling to put collateral agreements in place that would provide greater protection for the firm—a move they hoped would satisfy counterparties.

Up on the thirty-fifth floor, where Kim worked, phones had rung incessantly. Employees were glued to the Bear stock charts on their computer monitors, which were fed by an internal network. As if to alert them to the pending disaster, the feeds had failed intermittently throughout the day, at times when the stock was hitting new lows. Frazzled by the workload and the stress of not knowing what might happen to their company, employees argued openly.

By Friday Kim was so exhausted, he had told his wife he needed a break and took a personal day. But shortly after lunch, the phone rang in his Summit, New Jersey, home. It was Kim's boss. She said she had just gotten an emergency order from the lawyer who oversaw their department. "We are to hold off everything we are doing right now," she explained, "and pull up contracts that would allow counterparties to default on us." She needed everyone on deck, including him, she added.

Kim hung up the phone and looked at his wife, Jessica. "What's wrong?" she asked. "Jess, I have to go in now," he said. "And I can't take the train—you have to drive me." Waiting around at the train station, he worried, would take too long.

The couple packed their two small children into the car and began driving. Kim couldn't believe how swiftly the situation had escalated. "I hope we don't go under," he told Jessica. "I'll probably come home late, so don't wait up."

When he arrived, the legal department was in chaos. Printers were jamming and paper was running out as lawyers scrambled to read thousands of pages of counterparty agreements on every derivative product that Bear traded—commodities, swaps, options, even weather derivatives. Their goal was to identify "rating triggers" that, in the event of a downgrade, would allow counterparties to call default on money or securities that they owed Bear. Kim and his team would look at those, then try to preempt the moves by asking for a grace period or renegotiating the trades. "At that point, we didn't know what hit us," Kim recalls.

Bob Upton was by now looking at draft press releases of Bear downgrades from Standard & Poor's and Moody's that had been faxed in the midafternoon. The company was now flirting with "junk" status, meaning it was no longer an investment-grade borrower. Moody's had lowered their long-term debt to Baa1, three notches above junk, and Standard & Poor's had knocked them down to BBB, one notch above junk. It was a humiliating comedown that would inevitably cause further obstacles to finding funding.

Upton called John Stacconi, who worked for him in the treasury division. Stuck in his office on the twenty-third floor, Stacconi was being crushed with demands for cash. Hedge fund redemption requests that day had been massive, and Bear was desperately short of funds. The firm was due to wire out more than $11 billion, but simply didn't have it to send. J.P. Morgan was supposed to be lending money but was holding collateral securities it would not give back, so Bear had nothing with which to raise new money. Yet it couldn't get the collateral back until it appeared with some cash.

Stacconi sounded like he was about to have a heart attack. "I think we need to shut down the wire," he said. Upton hung up and ran down the hall to Molinaro's office.

He interrupted the CFO, who was in a meeting with Metrick. "This place is a complete disaster," Upton said. "We've got to shut down the fucking wire. We can't wire any more money out today."

"John's pulling his hair out," he continued. "Collateral's everywhere. We've got $11 billion, $12 billion, of hedge fund collateral sitting to get out, and we don't have the cash."

Shutting the wire down was an almost unheard-of measure. Now, not only was Bear contemplating a nuclear option, there wasn't even time to alert the Fed or the SEC.

Molinaro was calm. "Do what you have to do," he said.

4:00 P.M.

A couple of hours later, Geithner checked in with Hank Paulson. After hearing about the Bear investor call and conferring with Schwartz again that day, he was concerned that there was a perception problem. With the continued exodus of clients and the new crimps on raising loan money, he saw no way the company could last much beyond the weekend.

Yet Schwartz was indicating to investors that the Fed money would really last the twenty-eight days. "Alan still doesn't get it," Geithner told Paulson. "I think he's in denial."

Paulson, who was hearing the same, concurred. Schwartz couldn't go on thinking he had a month to seek the highest offer; he needed a white knight to come in that weekend, or again face bankruptcy. The regulators would have to set him straight.

7:00 P.M.

Molinaro spent the afternoon in triage mode, answering what calls he could and trying his best to answer questions about the implications of the facility. The stock was in freefall, and had closed for the day at $30—a 50 percent drop from the prior day's level. Nothing, it seemed, could reassure the market.

By nightfall, he was ready to drop. The markets had been closed for hours, and he was due back at the firm early Saturday morning to help J.P. Morgan's due diligence team. Wearily, he got in the car and began the slow journey back to New Canaan on a New York Friday night. He would probably miss dinner with his wife and younger children, but at least he could relax and finally get a little sleep.

Schwartz, who used a driver, was also en route to Connecticut.

Even for a self-described conciliator, the past few days had been unlike any Schwartz had ever experienced. He'd been through tough client situations before, advising corporate CEOs on hostile takeovers and how to deal with ornery shareholders. He'd seen deals done at lowball prices and frustrated executives driven out of their jobs unfairly. But never had his own firm been at the center of such a storm.

It wasn't that Schwartz thought Bear was invulnerable. He knew the market was a fickle beast, and that his employer was scrappy and undiversified relative to its peers. Industry competitors had long questioned why Schwartz stayed at such a lean and undistinguished investment bank, in which he was clearly the star player. "Alan is the finest boutique in the Bear Stearns mall," Bear's competitors would occasionally say. Many thought a man of Schwartz's talents deserved a platform like Morgan Stanley or Goldman Sachs, where an array of top deal makers would draw in the big clients, and the firms could present the capital raising and lending services that deep-pocketed companies demanded. But they had also seen Bear's investment bank blossom under Schwartz, who took deep satisfaction in growing his small shop into a more respected player.

Schwartz liked his team and his firm. He was comfortable there. He took pride in attending banking "bake-offs," in which each investment bank sent teams of bankers to pitch a potential client, and realizing he was the most senior representative there from any firm. He had a close relationship with many CEOs and CFOs, including Disney CEO Bob Iger, Verizon Communications CEO Ivan Seidenberg, Time Warner CEO Dick Parsons, and the Dolan family that ran Cablevision. Just this year, he had won a spot advising Microsoft in its bid to take over Yahoo. It was a hot ticket in a moribund deal market, and because of Schwartz, Bear was involved.

Like many of Bear's heavy hitters, Schwartz had grown up a scrapper. Born in Bay Ridge, Brooklyn, to parents who had never attended college, he came from a family with limited resources. He was the middle child in a family of three boys, a role that schooled him in the importance of getting along with others.

When Schwartz was a toddler, the family moved from Brooklyn to a modest home in suburban Levittown, New York, on the southern part of Long Island. Schwartz was raised there, playing sports in the street with other boys in the neighborhood and attending the nearby public schools. He played everything, but particularly loved baseball, where he had a talent for pitching.

Schwartz's father, Walter, worked as a traveling salesman. He later tried to start his own finance company, but it barely got off the ground. His mother mostly stayed at home, but from time to time she'd take on different jobs to help with the family's resources. One was as a bookkeeper at a local bowling alley.

As a student at General Douglas MacArthur High School, Schwartz won a baseball scholarship to Duke University. He had already been drafted to play professional ball, but wanted to focus on his education.

In 1968, he moved to Durham. He worked hard in school, making the academic honor roll as he pitched for Duke's varsity team. He joined a fraternity, Pi Kappa Alpha, and again attracted national notice for his baseball game. In his senior year of college, Schwartz was drafted by the Cincinnati Reds, but an elbow injury prevented him from joining the team.

Schwartz began working in Bear's Dallas office in 1976, just a few years out of school, as an institutional sales manager. In the years that followed, he helped devise investment strategies for mutual funds and other large clients, and ran investment research for a time. He moved to New York and became an investment banker shortly thereafter.

In the early 1980s, Schwartz married his first wife, Kathy. Their first child, a daughter, was born a year later.

By 1985, Schwartz had been named Bear's head of investment banking. Over time, he developed another successful tactic: sourcing a potential client's CFO. Unlike the CEO, who had broader strategic issues to worry about, the CFO was the executive who really cared which investment bank priced a stock offering or raised debt. So Schwartz reasoned that CFO relationships might do as much, or more, to help his division's bottom line. His strategy was so successful that other firms began playing defense, telling their own bankers to get to know the CFOs of client companies, not just the top dogs.

Part of Schwartz's appeal was his diplomatic skills. Gene Sykes, the Goldman media banker, first befriended Schwartz in the mid-1990s, when the two were on opposite sides of a negotiation between two pharmaceutical companies. It was a hostile process, and the CEOs the bankers represented came to dislike each other immensely, but Sykes and Schwartz walked away friends.

Schwartz understood the importance of appearances, and he took pains to carve out a niche for Bear in the sectors it knew well: drug companies, real estate, defense, and especially media.

To showcase the firm's clients and make new contacts among the research and investor communities, he established Bear's annual media-industry conference in the late 1980s. In its early years, the gathering was dominated by investment bankers, who showed up to hear corporate luminaries speak about their businesses. It was a rare opportunity to schmooze with CEOs one-on-one. Of the major investment firms, only Paine Webber held a similar event.

At the time, Bear had no major media analyst. But in 1994, the firm hired a former CBS television producer named Ray Katz to cover the large media and entertainment companies in hopes of raising Bear's profile as a go-to place for quality investment research on the companies for which Schwartz and his team provided banking services.

Katz soon took control of the event, which traditionally had been held in October. But he soon noticed that the mutual-fund and other professional investment firm analysts who attended were having to squeeze Bear's media conference into their schedules between third-quarter earnings announcements from the companies they followed, so Katz pushed for a spring time frame to ease the burden. He also changed the conference venue, which had historically rotated between California, Arizona, and Florida, permanently to Florida to save analysts the trouble of rising at 4:15 A.M. to talk to their clients on the East Coast before the start of the day's trading. The number of sign-ups soon swelled to more than six hundred people.

The conference became an important branding event for Bear, which had struggled to compete in the investment banking world with larger, more diversified operations. So Schwartz and Katz continued to play with its format, hoping to find new and compelling draws. In the early 2000s, they initiated a series of "fireside chats" with media CEOs. Starting with Schwartz's question-and-answer session with media mogul Barry Diller, who at the time ran USA Network, the talks soon became a signature event.

Schwartz also displayed a sense of humor. One year, when the event was still occasionally held on the West Coast, he and Katz told their guests that they'd secured an important VIP as a surprise speaker for the evening's dinner. Keeping the details strictly under wraps, they hired actors to dress up as Secret Service agents with earpieces and installed metal detectors outside the banquet room. Security was strict; Sumner Redstone, the Viacom chairman, had shown up without his identifying badge and was turned away. Then, when the time came, Schwartz slapped a presidential seal on the podium and introduced William Jefferson Clinton—at which point a Clinton impersonator stepped out. His jokes were a huge hit.

Like all of Bear's senior executives, Schwartz made great money during the firm's bull run in the 2000s. He took home $16 million in bonus alone for the year 2006, and was one of Bear's single largest shareholders, after Cayne.

In 2000, Schwartz paid close to $3 million for a six-bedroom house in Purchase, New York, with a view of the Long Island Sound. Three years later, he upgraded to an even swankier dwelling in Greenwich, for which he paid more than $10 million. Located on seven acres, that house was eleven thousand square feet.

In 2002, a year after divorcing Kathy, Schwartz remarried. His new wife, Nancy Seaman, was a widow several years his junior with two children. An entrepreneur in her own right, she was chairman of Houlihan Lawrence, a large residential real-estate company with properties in many of the wealthier communities in Westchester and its environs north of Manhattan.

Much as he loved his firm, Schwartz had never expected to be named CEO. For years, he had enjoyed a close relationship with Spector, his co-head as president and chief operating officer, and had cheerfully left the running of the capital markets business to him. Spector was nearly ten years younger than Schwartz and far more ambitious. Particularly since his son, Adam, had been stricken with cancer as a young child, Schwartz had kept in mind the value of a work-life balance. Adam had survived, but the lessons were clear: be mindful of family and don't take the job too seriously. There had been times when Schwartz had gotten swept up in work, to be sure, but he tried to remember those priorities when things got tough.

The prior August, when Cayne moved to oust Spector, Schwartz argued vehemently against it. He felt that Spector was being singled out, and that the company was better off with him than without. But Cayne was unmovable. It wasn't until after Spector's heated departure that Schwartz realized just how much tension had surrounded him, and how many employees had been put off by Spector's sharp edges. Cayne may have been off playing golf at important moments, but that didn't excuse Spector's leaving work on a Thursday night to fly by private jet to Martha's Vineyard. Both executives, it appeared, had lost track of Greenberg's long-held work ethic.

In the months that followed, Schwartz tried valiantly to fill Spector's shoes. To brush up on the details of Bear's fixed-income positions, he met frequently with the traders of mortgages and other securities, questioning them about their holdings and strategies. He often used his old friend's seventh-floor office, which had remained unfilled. During risk-management meetings, Schwartz tried to referee the arguments between traders like Marano, who was uninterested in downsizing his portfolio, and hawks like Ace Greenberg and

Steve Meyer, who wanted inventory sales to go off immediately. "We've got to cut!" Greenberg would yell, as Marano grumbled. These were not fun discussions.

Schwartz's own view was that Bear shouldn't sell valuable assets at distressed prices. But in an increasingly troubled housing market, distressed prices were pretty much all that existed. So he turned his thoughts to a strategic partner for Bear, like Kohlberg Kravis Roberts & Co. or PIMCO. In August and September, both held discussions with Schwartz and his team, but neither deal came together. Instead, Bear focused on a strategic partnership they'd been discussing with the Chinese investment bank CITIC Securities International. Later, the firm also hired Gary Parr to begin exploring similar tie-ups in the Middle East.

Back then, it was seven months before Bear would run out of cash, and the firm's future prospects seemed fair. Stocks rallied late that September and early October, and even Bear shares were temporarily lifted. But all was not well inside. Cayne had been hospitalized with a serious prostate infection early in the fall, and his recovery had been slow, making him less engaged in day-to-day business than ever. Investors were starting to take note. Worse yet, reporters were, too.

On November 1, the *Wall Street Journal* ran a devastating cover story on Cayne's distracted leadership. Entitled "Bear CEO's Handling of Crisis Raises Issues," the article discussed in detail Cayne's many absences from work during the events of the past summer, when the two hedge funds had failed. He had been out of the office at least ten out of the twenty-one working days that July, the article pointed out, when the funds had ultimately collapsed. He was in Nashville, Tennessee, for a big chunk of that time, competing in a bridge tournament and had made a habit of spending much of his Fridays on the golf course in Deal, New Jersey—without a cell phone or a BlackBerry.

Perhaps worst of all, the article made reference to Cayne's alleged marijuana use. During another bridge tournament in Memphis in 2004, the article stated, he had invited a woman and another event attendee into a lobby men's room at a Doubletree Hotel to share a joint with him. The incident, which Cayne denied, was evidence of his repeated use of pot, the article added.

For many of Bear's traders, the *Journal* article was the final, unacceptable blow to the firm in a string of public humiliations. A pot-smoking CEO at a time when Wall Street was under duress? they raged. Outrageous. Most were already furious about the prospect of receiving small or no bonuses for the year, appalled that the firm's fourth quarter was veering toward a loss, and had zero interest in tolerating a dithering seventy-three-year-old CEO for one minute longer.

At the year-end management meetings, fur flew. Marano and Meyer squabbled openly about pay, and many others began asking when Cayne would be replaced. Paul Friedman and some of his buddies began talking among themselves about holding a sit-in in Schwartz's office on the forty-second floor if Cayne wasn't forced out—soon. All stopped Schwartz in the hallway to air their grievances.

By the time the new year rolled around, the firm was practically in open revolt. Schwartz took a deep breath and went into Cayne's office. "Something's got to change," he said.

"Like what?" Cayne said.

"You've got to step down," Schwartz replied.

Cayne leaned back in his chair. There was a long silence. Aware of the dynamics around him, Cayne had told outside directors after the December board meeting that he planned to step down sometime in the near future. He hadn't set a date, but now circumstances appeared to be choosing one for him.

"I'm glad it was you who came," Cayne finally said.

After an emergency board meeting, Schwartz was promoted on January 8.

Cayne's removal may have settled the angst over Bear's leadership, but it did little to ebb concerns about its precarious market positions. Later in January, during a breakfast meeting on the twelfth floor with more than a dozen senior fixed-income managers, Schwartz laid out his vision for the company. Among other things, he explained, he had hired the consulting firm McKinsey & Company to help restructure the firm's top management, which had been dominated for too long by the small group of people on the executive and management committees. He wanted to bring fresher blood to the fore.

Acknowledging the pressure to bring in an outside investor or consider doing a deal with another company, Schwartz told the group that "all options [were] on the table." But he didn't want to be rash. If the time came when Bear Stearns appeared more vulnerable, he added, he would look more closely at possible deals.

During the question-and-answer session that followed, David Schoenthal, the hard-charging fifty-nine-year-old head of foreign-exchange trading, was the first to speak. He had been one of the guys calling for the sit-in to get rid of Cayne, and was now extremely concerned about Bear's cash positions. "This all sounds nice, Alan," he said, "but when are we going to raise capital?"

Schwartz stood firm. "We don't need more capital," he replied. Less than a year ago, he pointed out, when the firm's capital was north of $13 billion, some analysts had considered Bear Stearns's cash levels to be too high because the firm wasn't generating as high a return on equity—an important measure of an investment bank's performance—as some of its peers. For the moment, he was comfortable with the firm's capital levels of about $11.8 billion, he added.

However, the firm's sizable mortgage portfolio still posed a problem. "We've got to get this cleaned up," Schwartz had told traders around that time. Of the roughly $46 billion in mortgages and related securities the firm held, a significant chunk comprised "agency-

backed" securities, or securities tied to home loans guaranteed by
Fannie Mae and Freddie Mac. But Bear also held its share of "Alt-A"
mortgage loans, which were only one notch above the subprime in
quality, and a smattering of commercial mortgage-backed securities,
and a large collection of original commercial mortgage "whole"
loans, some of which were losing value.

As long as he was tinkering with the management structure,
Schwartz also wanted to shore up the firm's risk-management ap-
paratus. Late in 2007, he had hired a different consulting firm, Oliver
Wyman, to suggest ways to streamline the risk-management process
and bring the technology and oversight up to date.

That winter one of Bear Stearns's major clients and trading partners, the Newport Beach, California, money manager PIMCO, had
admonished senior fixed-income managers about the need for a
deeper cash cushion. Their warning—which had followed threats to
pull a big chunk of PIMCO business from the firm—had put the fear
of God in the managers, some of who now wanted to take matters
into their own hands.

In January, executives from the Japanese bank Sumitomo met in
New York with Schwartz and Molinaro. They had been talking to
Michel Peretié, the head of Bear Stearns's London office, and were
interested in a possible investment in the firm.

Sumitomo's healthy balance sheet and the chance to expand Bear
Stearns's small footprint in Asia were attractive. But the Japanese
bankers had a tough demand: that Schwartz cancel his pending deal
with CITIC, which was expected to close in the coming months,
bringing $1 billion in new capital.

A group of Bear managers met on January 10 to look over the
Sumitomo proposal. The bank was interested in taking a 10 to 30
percent stake, which appealed to worried traders. But Schwartz
couldn't get past the CITIC problem, and didn't see how the deal
could get done. "Let's stop kidding ourselves," he said, abruptly shutting the deal book. "This is never going to happen." He suggested

that Bear focus on doing some smaller transactions with Sumitomo instead to see if the two companies jelled.

In February, a similar proposal, this time from the Japanese securities firm Nomura Holdings, Inc., was also dismissed, as were on-again, off-again talks with the publicly traded hedge fund Fortress Investment Group about a possible purchase of the firm. Schwartz still wasn't convinced of the need for more capital, and the idea of Fortress management eventually running the combined companies was a turnoff.

By the beginning of March, when raw numbers from the first fiscal quarter became available, things were looking up. Bear appeared to have earned a profit of $1.23 per share—despite widespread markdowns in the value of mortgage securities held by the firm and many of its competitors. It had the lowest debt from leveraged loans, or loans made to corporate clients to help complete deals, of any of the major investment banks, Schwartz reasoned, and, unlike some others, Bear was not exposed to the complex mortgage-backed securities known as CDOs, which had been deemed highly dangerous because of the weakening assets to which they were tied.

Schwartz returned his attention to the management changes he was planning, which he intended to announce internally on March 25. Encouraged by the preliminary earnings results, he began preparing for the annual media conference, set to begin March 10 at the swanky Breakers hotel in Palm Beach, Florida.

It was the week before Bear would fail, and worrisome signs were already appearing. Days prior, the London hedge fund Peloton Partners LLP had collapsed, unable to secure enough cash to meet a flurry of margin calls—demands for more cash or collateral—from lenders. Bad buzz was also encircling Carlyle Capital Corporation, a London-based unit of the Washington, D.C., private equity firm Carlyle Group, which was said to be having margin problems as well. Similar problems were besetting Thornburg Mortgage, a home-loan provider to customers with good credit. As a lender and holder of mortgages with tentacles reaching throughout the financial system, Bear stood to lose money from all three.

Verizon's Seidenberg had invited Schwartz to speak at a board dinner on the evening of March 6 that was also to be held in Palm Beach. The Bear CEO was concerned about leaving town, but couldn't see any immediate reason to stay, so he went.

That Friday, Saturday, and Sunday, Schwartz made a number of calls from the Breakers. He spoke to both Warsh and Geithner. The cost of an insurance policy to protect against a default by Bear on its debt was skyrocketing—a worrisome sign.

On March 10, the first day of the media conference, Schwartz woke up to bad news. The Fed had launched a $50 billion lending facility intended to provide needed cash to troubled financial institutions through the purchase of assets, including home loans. Separately, a major rating agency had downgraded a swath of Alt-A mortgages packaged into securities by Bear, deeming them too risky for conservative investors. The firm's shares were getting hammered; investors seemed to be interpreting the Fed's move as an attempted bailout of Bear, and the rating change on the securities as a downgrade of the firm itself. The week only got worse from there.

Now, at the tail end of the worst day of his professional life, Schwartz was somewhere south of Greenwich when he got an unexpected call from Paulson and Geithner. There appeared to be some confusion about the time frame attached to the Fed loan, the officials explained. The funds would remain in place only until the Asian markets opened on Sunday night, New York time—not for a month, as the press release had implied. "You need to have a deal by Sunday night," Paulson said.

The day had turned into a bloodbath, the Treasury secretary felt. If anything, creditor confidence appeared to have sunk with the early-morning announcement, and the rating agency downgrades had made matters far worse. He wished that he or Geithner had thought to call the agencies and urge prudence, but it was too late to do that now. Counterparties had realized the Fed loan was nothing more than a temporary bridge, and they'd no doubt destroy what was left of Bear on Monday. Without a weekend acquisition, a massive point drop in the Dow was probably inevitable, along with the quick failures not only of Bear but of the weaker investment banks that were also struggling with large mortgage exposures and questionable risk management—among them Lehman, Merrill Lynch, and maybe even Morgan Stanley. The situation was unthinkably bad.

Schwartz felt numb. He had thought he had a month, and suddenly he had two days. But there was little he could say to argue. This was the federal government, after all, and Bear was now on the hook for billions of dollars thanks to their generosity. He told the officials he understood and hung up.

Molinaro was stopped at a gas station on the Merritt Parkway for a cup of coffee when his cell phone rang. It was Schwartz, who quickly conveyed the bad news.

"You gotta be fucking kidding me," Molinaro said. "They're going to pull the plug on us over the weekend?"

Schwartz recapped the conversation. Paulson had said that enough was enough. He wouldn't stay up another night, all night, worrying about Bear Stearns. He had reminded Schwartz of their conversation early that morning in which he had asked the CEO if he really wanted to accept the government's money knowing that Bear's future would no longer be in his hands. Yes, Schwartz had said, he remembered. This is going to end this weekend, Paulson had replied.

Molinaro, still exhausted, couldn't believe it. We have no friends, he thought. And, unlike some firms, Bear is not too big to fail. He climbed back into the car and finished the drive home.

8:00 P.M.

After his awkward phone call with Geithner and Schwartz, Hank Paulson had gone downtown to the National Geographic Society building on M Street. He and his wife were donors to the organization, and Paulson had promised her they could attend a screening that night of a film called *Lord God Bird,* about the rare ivory-billed woodpecker.

Sitting in the theater, the Treasury secretary regretted his decision. What am I doing here? he wondered. During the social hour afterward, he was too preoccupied to converse much with the other donors. Wendy was annoyed. "You're barely acknowledging people," she told him.

Ever since the company's cash crisis had reared its head the prior August, Paul Friedman had had a terrible time sleeping. He would nod off easily, only to wake up around one or two o'clock in the morning filled with anxiety. Sometimes he'd lie in bed just staring at the ceiling. If he was restless enough, he'd get up, pace the house, maybe page through a magazine until he got sleepy again. He spent hours surfing the Web, watching YouTube videos to pass the time and finding the images mesmerizing.

Sunday nights became a torment. Fearful of what might happen to Bear the next week, Friedman would try to stretch out the weekend as long as possible, thinking that if it wasn't yet Monday, nothing bad could happen. He'd stay up late in the family room of his Scarsdale house, watching old movies on television until he couldn't fight off the exhaustion any longer. After a night like that, Steve Begleiter, the firm's head of corporate strategy, was usually his first call of the day. "Have we sold the company yet?" Friedman would ask. The answer—even during the weeks when suitors had been hanging around—was always no.

When Friedman got home on Friday, he was beyond weary, and knew he needed a solid night's sleep in order to face the J.P. Morgan and Flowers teams the next day. He took an Ambien from a stash he usually reserved for long-haul flights and turned in around eight.

An hour later, Susie shook him awake. Tim Greene was on the phone, and it was urgent.

Friedman took the phone and groggily said hello. Greene was befuddled. He had spent the last several hours trying to negotiate the terms of a $7 billion loan from J.P. Morgan, he explained, and the bank had just informed him that the lending facility Bear executives had thought would last for twenty-eight days was in fact good only through the weekend. Greene didn't want to sign the company's future away, he said, but if he didn't agree to those terms, J.P. Morgan wouldn't give Bear the money. "What should I do?" he asked.

In his drugged state, Friedman was having some trouble thinking straight. Still, the whole thing struck him as odd, given that as Bear's clearing agent, J.P. Morgan was the ultimate recipient of any loans to Bear anyway. "They're basically lending to themselves," Friedman mused aloud, wondering why J.P. Morgan was giving Greene so much trouble. "Call the Fed," he finally said.

Greene explained that he and a Bear compliance lawyer had just hung up with Geithner's chief of staff, who had told the Bear executives to go along with whatever J.P. Morgan wanted.

"This is way above my pay grade," Friedman replied. "Patch in Alan—and Mike Solender," he added, invoking Bear's general counsel.

"We tried," said Greene. But Solender, whom he said had also taken a sleeping pill that night, was too sleepy to stay on the phone; midway through the conversation, he had started snoring.

With Friedman holding on the line, Greene dialed Schwartz, who was by then at home as well. Again the repo trader explained the situation: the abrupt change in the timeline of the loan facility, J.P. Morgan's refusal to lend the money if the documents weren't signed, and Geithner's desire to stay out of it. Schwartz was exasperated. "It doesn't make any difference," he told Greene. "Just sign the fucking document."

Friedman was leery. "Are you sure?" he asked Schwartz.

"Yes," Schwartz said.

There was a pregnant pause as all three realized how short a lifeline they were facing. "Well, Timmy, I guess you have your instructions," Friedman finally said. They all hung up.

Except for Schwartz himself, the board had no idea what a vise Bear was in. Late that night, Tese spoke to Sam Molinaro. There was some funny stuff going on with the Fed's deadline, the CFO explained. He wanted Tese and Salerno to huddle with him and Schwartz the next morning to discuss it in person. They might still be able to work out a plan for saving the company, but it would have to be the fastest corporate deal in Bear history.

SATURDAY
March 15, 2008

Midnight

While two of Bear's managers had lapsed into a drug-induced sleep, others couldn't get their minds off the company's worsening situation.

Peter Bainlardi, who ran one of the fixed-income division's trading desks, fired off an e-mail at 12:26 A.M. Saturday morning that summed up how most of Bear's senior traders and managers were feeling.

"Plan to Save Bear Stearns—Important—Please Read" was addressed to Schwartz, Marano, Mayer, and other top players in the fixed-income division. Written on Bainlardi's laptop at his downtown Manhattan apartment, it was a long and heartfelt meditation on the bind Bear found itself in and what might be done to extricate the firm.

"We find ourselves in the weakest position possible—we can't help feeling like this has somehow been plotted against us, and in a way, it's in the interest of the large commercial banks to see us fail," he wrote.

Bainlardi, along with many others, had clearly been hearing the conspiracy theories about Bear's targeting by short sellers and competitors to be the butt of negative rumors. Some, they speculated, wanted to make money by betting that Bear's shares would fall and then reaping the benefits once they did; others might be interested in purchasing Bear at a fire-sale price that wouldn't be available under better circumstances. If Bear failed, went the reasoning, it would also point up the relative strength of bigger players like J.P. Morgan and Citigroup—large commercial banks with far bigger balance sheets and less risk-intensive businesses. Citi, it turned out, was already hobbled by its own huge trading losses and a bloated cost structure, so only J.P. Morgan stood to benefit from Bear's demise.

Bainlardi also pointed out that J.P. Morgan seemed to have an unfair advantage. The bank, he felt, could essentially swoop in during a weekend and snatch up either the entire company or its prized portions on the cheap. And it would be able to do so with backing from the government, a low price, and little risk of its own.

"This makes no sense!" he wrote. "The Fed only cares about the large commercial banks," he added, in a nod to the fact that the Federal Reserve regulated only the firms that had customer deposits, not the investment banks like Bear, which were overseen by the SEC. "Protecting them is the key to saving the U.S. economic system—the over leveraged investment banks are in the way in their view."

It was true that the Fed's Friday-morning loan, offered through J.P. Morgan, had had a devastating effect, doing nothing to assuage nervous stockholders, clients, or lenders. And the Bear managers had no idea what the Fed's motivations were. Of course the central bank cared more about systemic risk than about the fortunes of any particular bank. But there was no evidence that the Fed was favoring J.P. Morgan over other bidders, and what happened in the wake of its temporary credit facility had been beyond its control. It was unfortunate that the stopgap funding it had provided had, in fact, queered some of Bear's creditors. But it was their right to back out of deals or refuse to refresh credit if they thought the borrower was simply too unreliable to pay them back.

By sending his SOS, Bainlardi gave its recipients a pointed reminder of the unenviable situation they were in. Bear was in deep trouble. It had been victimized by careless gossip, predatory behavior, or both. It was lurching toward an unwinnable one-party fire sale, and a solution was needed urgently. And Bainlardi didn't even know at that point that the twenty-eight-day period had turned into two days.

7:00 A.M.

Six and a half hours later, the alarm rang in Paul Friedman's Scarsdale bedroom. Even a dose of Ambien hadn't prevented him from being interrupted by calls the night before, and he was not feeling refreshed. But there would be no sleeping in that day. Time to get up and go back to work, he thought as he trudged down the hall to take a shower.

Friedman skipped breakfast and climbed into his gray Audi, which was parked in the two-car garage of his rambling house. Built in a quiet, leafy cul-de-sac, it was the sort of place he and Susie could only dream of when he'd started at Bear back in the 1970s. He remembered when he'd been promoted to senior managing director in 1991. To attend the celebratory dinner at the Rainbow Room, the exclusive restaurant high above New York's Rockefeller Center in Midtown, Susie had spent more than $200 on a two-piece outfit—and then only after her mother had talked her into it.

Still, the Friedmans didn't take their money for granted. That prior summer, they'd had a hard talk about what would happen if Bear went down, taking Paul's bonus and stock holdings with it. In the interest of caution, he had opened an account with HSBC and moved some money offshore. But he was leery of doing anything with his Bear stock; his intimate knowledge of the company's health could have sparked questions about insider trading.

Driving down the Hutchinson River Parkway toward Manhattan this morning, Friedman felt a strange sense of relief. His worst fears were coming true—Bear was on its knees, and it wasn't at all clear that a solution would emerge this weekend. Yet at least things were finally moving toward some sort of conclusion. After nine months of feeling sick with worry, he couldn't take the stress any longer. Now he knew for a fact that Bear would be either alive or dead in about thirty-six hours—end of story.

The orders for Saturday morning had been straightforward: Meet at Bear's conference center and be ready to answer J.P. Morgan's questions; tell them everything there is to know, because Bear needs a deal this weekend, and they are the best possible option.

Around 8:00, Friedman pulled the Audi into his usual lot on Forty-sixth Street, where Bear employees had a discount. He headed toward the building.

While Friedman was driving in, Schwartz was on the phone giving the independent directors Vincent Tese and Fred Salerno, who were still at their vacation homes in Florida, an update on what had happened during his commute home the previous night. Schwartz explained that the Fed had delivered a forty-eight-hour deadline, and that a deal would have to be accomplished that weekend or the company, more than likely, would go bust.

Neither Tese nor Salerno was surprised at the move. Tese was experienced in both the private and public sectors. He was a retired lawyer who had for a time been vice chairman of the Port Authority of New York and New Jersey. In the 1980s and early 1990s, he had also served as New York State's superintendent of banks, and had seen banks fighting for their survival before. In Tese's opinion, the Fed was an apolitical player; all it cared about was the safety of the system. Once the Fed thought a bank was gravely wounded, it wanted fast solutions. The Treasury, he thought, was another story. Its officials weren't above politics. And if Hank Paulson had an agenda here, it wouldn't surprise him.

Tese remembered an experience he'd had in 1985, when as banking superintendent he faced the likely failure of the Bowery Savings Bank in New York City. Alan Greenspan, later the Federal Reserve chairman, had been on the board of Bowery at the time.

The bank had been operating at a loss and wanted a government rescue. Unsure what its future held, Tese issued his own ultimatum: Either close or we'll sell you. The market couldn't afford for Bowery Savings to languish in uncertainty, and it was sold to a consortium of private investors in short order. He figured something like that would now happen here.

Listening to the call was the Sullivan banking expert Rodge Cohen, who was in his own car en route to the city from his home in Irvington, New York. Having spent the past two mornings meeting with officials in Washington, he had already heard hints that Bear might be given less than a month to work with. Fed officials had made it clear to him on Friday that they wanted a very quick resolution to Bear's problem—not a lingering, open-ended drama. Treasury people had made similar comments that morning. It was as if they were preemptively letting the financial world know that they didn't take kindly to the idea of a government rescue.

8:30 A.M.

By 8:30 that morning, Bear's top management had gathered on the twelfth floor of 383 Madison Avenue for their meetings with J.P. Morgan. Bagels, croissants, juice, and coffee had been laid out, and people were milling around, making small talk, as they picked at the spread of food. Since it was a Saturday, most of the men were wearing khakis and blazers.

Unlike on Friday, when a sense of shock and anger had prevailed, the mood was one of reluctant acceptance. Bear's once-scrappy employees knew their company was in peril, and the best they could do now was to edge it toward the best possible sale to another firm. If that firm was J.P. Morgan, then so be it. It was better than losing jobs and stock holdings in a total wipeout.

The gathering was a who's who of senior talent at Bear: Schwartz, Molinaro, Upton, Marano, Friedman, Steve Meyer, and Bruce Lisman—the two heads of Bear's equities department, as well as its top prime-brokerage unit executives. There was also a smattering of junior employees, some straight out of college, who had been called in to help with the scut work, like doing data runs on computers and carrying documents from one meeting to another.

Eventually Schwartz gathered the fifty- to sixty-person team together in order to make a short speech. He, too, seemed calm and focused.

"I want to thank everybody for coming in," he said. "The last few days have been very difficult for everybody, but we're here to get through the weekend with a view to getting a transaction done. It has to be done this weekend." He didn't mention the new two-day deadline, but he didn't need to—anyone who'd been at work on Friday understood firsthand what a precarious position Bear was in.

With that, smaller groups were dispatched to their assigned areas on the twelfth and thirteenth floors, where a number of conference rooms had been prepared for the due-diligence meetings. It was going to be another long day.

9:00 A.M.

Molinaro, Schwartz, Metrick, and Bear general counsel Mike Solender, who was by now wide awake, gathered in a large dining room on the twelfth floor to face J.P. Morgan's top brass: Steve Black, Doug Braunstein, the bank's top dealmaker, and Steve Cutler, the J.P. Morgan general counsel who had once run the enforcement division of the SEC. Bill Winters, Black's cochief in the investment bank, dialed in from London, where he lived. He was due to fly back on Sunday.

Once pleasantries were exchanged, Molinaro launched into an overview of Bear's business. He discussed the firm's expenses and revenues and reviewed the preliminary numbers he had compiled on the first quarter, which had ended February 29. Despite the embarrassing loss during the fourth quarter of 2007—the first ever in Bear's profitable eighty-five-year history—the figures indicated that Bear had made well north of $1 per share for the first three months of the fiscal year.*

Molinaro talked briefly about the firm's key business units, and the state of each. It was the same presentation he'd given hundreds of times to investors and analysts—albeit, without the not-yet-released earnings materials.

Black was the chief spokesman on the J.P. Morgan side, and the Bear team was impressed with his cordiality. He was receptive to the information, they felt, and showed a genuine interest in getting something done. They were relieved. It was hard enough to show up for the events of that day, and J.P. Morgan's team was making things easier by showing some deference. They understand how high the stakes are, Molinaro mused to himself.

When the meeting broke up, he and Schwartz took Black into a smaller room for a more private discussion. There the Bear executives went into detail about their top people, and told them who was who in the company and what their chief concerns were within Bear's businesses. They also discussed the two-day timetable. Unlike Friday, when things had been moving at a more leisurely pace, they explained, Bear was now in a position of needing to close a deal by Sunday night. The firm was under government orders to do so.

Black thanked the executives for their time and promised to be in touch. Molinaro and Schwartz returned to their own offices to check messages and start working the phones.

At the same time, groups of managers were meeting in the thirteenth-floor conference center with their counterparts from across the street, discussing the state of Bear's various divisions with the people they'd potentially be working for at J.P. Morgan. Tom

---

*Those figures were preliminary. Bear's actual first-quarter earnings, disclosed later in a regulatory filing, came to $.89.

Marano and his mortgage team sat in a room with J.P. Morgan's mortgage traders, and Upton and his staff sat with a group from J.P. Morgan's treasury division. In yet another room, the top players in Bear's equities division sat with Emily Portney, the chief financial officer of that unit at J.P. Morgan. Her boss, Carlos Hernandez, was traveling in Egypt, so she ran the meeting in his stead.

Portney introduced herself and asked for an overview of the business. Steve Meyer, who had just returned from an aborted holiday in Lake Tahoe with his wife and kids, took over. For three hours, he and his team walked the J.P. Morgan attendees through their business, disclosing how much cash and collateral it had on hand and what some of its major positions were. If a topic seemed to require a more detailed explanation, smaller groups would leave the room and talk privately in the corridor.

Portney and her colleagues were impressed with the Bear group's friendly, obliging tone. But certain questions about risk and clients made Meyer's people uncomfortable. Even though J.P. Morgan had signed a nondisclosure, or "confidentiality," agreement that would keep the details of such conversations under wraps, the Bear equities managers weren't accustomed to telling competitors about their big accounts. They still had a sneaking fear that the deal talks would fall apart, leaving J.P. Morgan with juicy details about Bear's most important clients. So in some of the side conversations that took place in the hallways, they waffled on a number of questions, telling J.P. Morgan they didn't know the answers to everything they wanted to know.

Tim Geithner had a meeting of his own that morning. Faced with a situation far beyond his personal experience, he sought out the advice of a gray-haired eminence: Paul Volcker, the eighty-one-year-old former Fed chairman who had run the central bank for nearly twenty years.

Talking in Volcker's Manhattan residence, Geithner presented the ugly picture: Bear was likely to fail without a deal and the best possible acquirer appeared to be J.P. Morgan. "I think we might be able to put a deal together," the Fed bank president explained. They talked it through. "That sounds like a good idea," Volcker agreed.

11:00 A.M.

Paulson also got going early on Saturday. Still ensconced in his Washington home, he began making a round of phone calls. He and Geithner had agreed to divide and conquer in handling the various parties: Geithner would keep in touch with both Bear and J.P. Morgan throughout the day, and Paulson would help canvass possible acquirers. In between, the government officials would connect to give each other updates, looping in Bernanke and others as necessary.

Late that morning, Paulson and Geithner held a call with Schwartz, Cohen, and Bear's investment banker Gary Parr. Together, they compared notes on the potential interested parties and where things stood.

Deutsche Bank immediately came up. Geithner had talked to the bank's chairman, Josef Ackermann, in the past, and he seemed to have an appetite for doing deals. Paulson, who knew Ackermann from his years at Goldman, offered to call him personally.

Parr, however, wasn't sure Deutsche would bite. He had talked to a senior person in Deutsche's U.S. operations the day before, and the executive had seemed quite hesitant. Deutsche believed Bear had some good assets, the executive had said, but it would be hard to assess all the risks in a single weekend. He vowed to try to pull a team of surveyors together, but had made no promises about what they could accomplish.

On Friday, Parr had also spoken to the chiefs of the Bank of New York Mellon and the Royal Bank of Canada. Both had seemed interested, but by early Saturday morning, both had fallen away. The problem was twofold, as they explained it: Neither was interested in buying the whole firm, but only the bits and pieces that filled holes in their own companies. And the whole situation was moving too quickly; neither could get comfortable with a firm rumored to be deeply in trouble in the course of just forty-eight hours.

Parr was disappointed, but he could hardly blame them. It was a refrain he'd hear over and over as he scanned the market for interested parties that day.

Some other contenders had been ruled out preemptively. Because of CEO Ken Griffin's calls, Parr and Schwartz knew of Citadel's interest in a quick purchase; he was only too eager to send a team in from Chicago to get a look at Bear's books. But the Bear team had doubts about whether Citadel could close a deal for the much larger firm under such extreme time pressure. Citadel's previous investments, like the stock trader E*TRADE, had involved much smaller-scale operations. Moreover, Citadel, a mysterious, privately held entity controlled firmly by the thirty-nine-year-old Griffin, was rumored to be shorting Bear stock—essentially betting that it would fall and make money as it did. Fair or unfair, Bear executives had little time for companies that might be profiting as Bear's stock tumbled. Given their own doubts, they felt that Citadel lacked the seal of approval that a bigger or more widely understood acquirer might bring, and that Bear so desperately needed this weekend.

J.C. Flowers, however, was very much in the mix. Having returned to New York late on Thursday, Chris Flowers had dispatched a team of people to 383 to begin due diligence on Friday, and the same group had returned Saturday morning for another round of discussions. As J.P. Morgan teams worked upstairs in the dining and conference centers, Flowers was squirreled away on the executive floor below, spread out in and around Cayne's empty office.

That morning, Flowers and Parr had divided up a list of investors to contact, hoping that each of their personal relationships with buyers might come in handy. If Flowers were to do a deal, his firm was prepared to invest about $3 billion in Bear in exchange for a large stake of the company. But he needed an additional $20 billion or so in order to absorb Bear's costs and potential trading losses, as well as to reassure Bear's trading partners that it could make good on future trades. He was now swiftly trying to compile a list of such backers.

On Flowers's list of parties to call was a handful of sovereign funds, or investment pools run by foreign governments: the large Spanish bank Santander; a group of Japanese institutions that Flowers knew well from his past ventures in Asia; and Warren Buffett.

Parr was following up with the parties he'd called yesterday, as well as a few new ones. His pitch had broadened. Rather than simply asking investors if they'd like to buy Bear outright or make a large investment, as he had on Thursday night, he was now listing an array of different options, including a purchase of just one or more major assets, like Bear's prime-brokerage arm.

He was grateful for the help from Flowers, and relieved that at least one other party was in the mix to compete with J.P. Morgan. Multiple bidders would certainly spur more price competition than a single one.

However, back on the late-morning call, Paulson expressed his doubts about the Flowers bid. He wanted to know that there was strong capital behind the proposal—either a single big bank or a consortium of banks—before he was going to spend much time considering it. Nobody but a bank with a huge balance sheet could absorb the liabilities that would come along with a Bear purchase, Paulson reasoned—certainly not a small private-equity shop that was trying to drum up tens of billions of dollars in backing on the fly. Still, he didn't want to rule them out; Bear needed all the options it could get.

Paulson's thinking was logical enough, but there was a tense his-

tory between the two men. A star investment banker at Goldman
Sachs with a twenty-year career there, Flowers had founded the firm's
wildly successful financial-institutions group, which provided advisory help to banks, brokers, and insurance companies considering
mergers, IPOs, and acquisitions, and was deeply respected in the
markets. His group worked on some of the biggest takeovers of the
1990s, earning tens of millions of dollars in banking fees in the process. On his watch, Goldman advised on the $61.6 billion combina-
tion of NationsBank and Bank of America and the $34.4 billion
purchase of Wells Fargo by Norwest.

Flowers, a wiry, bespectacled Bostonian, also counseled Goldman on its own initial public offering plans at a time when some of
its 190 partners were wary of the idea. He pored over the firm's books
and records, building a strong case for floating shares to the public
to take on fresh capital, establish a currency for making acquisitions,
and grow the firm beyond its 11,400-person size. Eventually, the
group voted in favor of the offering, which was undertaken in the
spring of 1999.

But when it came to being promoted, Flowers had been passed over
by Paulson and Corzine, who were then running Goldman as a team.
Just months before the firm's scheduled IPO, Flowers was denied one
of the three spots as cochief operating officers of the firm's investment-
banking division; he was also passed over for a spot on the management committee. So, at the ripe age of forty, he informed Goldman's
executive committee of his plans to retire. "I've done so many deals
that doing the next deal isn't that important to me," he said in an interview just two months before announcing his departure.

During the intervening years, he struck out on his own. In 2000,
he and another private-equity investor convinced the Japanese government to let them buy the struggling Asian financial-services firm
Long-Term Credit Bank for $1.2 billion out of bankruptcy. They im-
mediately went to work slashing costs, restructuring, and creating
new strategies. The resultant company, renamed Shinsei Bank, gen-

erated hundreds of millions of dollars in profit for the investors through its IPO in 2004.

By then, Flowers had opened his eponymous private-equity shop, known as J.C. Flowers & Co., and had lured a couple of former Goldman partners to join him. The group pursued financial acquisitions with vigor, buying a unit of the insurance giant Conseco out of bankruptcy for $850 million and the investment-banking boutique Fox-Pitt Kelton for an undisclosed price.

Some deals, however, didn't come together. In 2005, Flowers's firm failed in its effort to be the lead investor in the futures trading business of the defunct commodities firm Refco for $768 million. Then, in 2007, a deal to invest in the struggling student lender Sallie Mae collapsed after a fight over the price of the company that was so acrimonious it wound up in court. That August, Flowers had looked at Bear, too, sending a team of people to meet with firm managers during the troubled time after Warren Spector had been booted. But the Bear group had been turned off by their suitors, feeling they were in it for a cheap acquisition rather than a heartfelt commitment to turn the business around.

Flowers was at Bear that morning, working his own way down a list of investors in Cayne's sixth-floor office. Despite his personal wealth, Flowers was strikingly casual, always sporting a digital running watch and, in milder months, a Barbour hunting jacket. His straight-talking style, too, fit in well with the culture at Bear.

His firm was prepared to put $3 billion into Bear, or between $2 and $3 per share. But he felt any deal would be imprudent without the backing of some major financial institutions.

Cayne was late to the board's 11:00 A.M. call that morning, and Ace Greenberg was angry. As soon as Cayne came on the line, Greenberg asked if he'd been delayed at the bridge table. Cayne said no.

The two then began to argue about whether Cayne should return to New York for the next two days' deliberations, rather than stay where he was and participate telephonically. Cayne didn't want to leave. "It's very difficult," he told the directors. "Why do I have to come back? I can do it by phone."*

"We can't afford to have another story that you're playing bridge at this time," Greenberg snapped. In fact, a blog item on the *Wall Street Journal*'s Web site had already pointed out that Cayne had spent Thursday and Friday competing in Detroit while the company flailed—complete with comparisons between Cayne's performance at the bridge table and Bear's stock price. Now the paper was tracking whether or not Cayne returned for the weekend's discussions.

To those listening, Greenberg sounded adamant. After years of being shunted aside by Cayne, the enmity between the two former CEOs, long kept under wraps in board and executive meetings, was emerging in force.

Schwartz took the floor. In all probability, he said, the company would need to be sold in two days. He was "shocked" by the government's change of heart, he said, but there was no point in arguing now. They had to get on with their talks with J.P. Morgan, Flowers, and any other suitors who might present themselves.

One of the directors asked if there was any way to fight the ultimatum.

Rodge Cohen, sitting in his downtown office, spoke up. There was no way to fight the government, he told the group. He knew from experience that they would not keep Bear afloat. There was no choice but to proceed with the due-diligence process and hope for the best.

Bear's worsening situation reminded him of something he'd been through in 1984, when Continental Illinois National Bank and Trust Company had weathered a bank run. Spooked by a stockpile of bad loans the bank had purchased from another bank that failed, de-

---

*Cayne says through a representative that he proactively decided to come back and that he was not prodded by Greenberg.

positors abruptly pulled $10 billion out of Continental Illinois, then the country's seventh-largest bank. Within just a few days that May, the bank was teetering on the brink of insolvency.

Government regulators were alarmed. Deeming Conti Illinois, as it was known, "too big to fail," the Federal Deposit Insurance Corporation pledged $4.5 billion to stabilize the situation. Shareholders were ultimately wiped out as the company's stock price plummeted, but bondholders were protected, and the bank lived.

As a midlevel partner in Sullivan & Cromwell's banking practice, Cohen spent a good deal of time working with Dave Taylor, the executive who was brought in to become chairman of the rescued bank. The lesson he took from the crisis was that a financial institution can withstand a devastating liquidity run—but only with intervention from the government. And once the regulators took over, Cohen noted, the firm's original management and structure were unlikely to survive.

Alan "Ace" Greenberg had never been known to mince words.* Short, portly, and bald except for a few whisps of closely cropped white hair behind his ears, Greenberg, now eighty, neither looked nor acted the part of a Wall Street big shot. His personal interests included bridge, magic tricks, yo-yos, and teaching tricks to dogs. At work, he espoused a uniquely democratic system in which his desk was mixed in with those of other stock traders, and anyone, regardless of rank, was invited to come to him with concerns or complaints. He often dealt with miscreants on the trading desk personally, chewing out those who made careless errors and firing those who lied about them. No issue was too small for his consideration, especially if it affected the firm's profit margins or its image.

As head of the firm from 1978 to 1993, he hated wasting time. Colleagues found him grouchy. He returned phone calls within

---

*Ace Greenberg declined to comment on the details of his tenure at Bear.

twenty-four hours, but often limited the other party to just one or two questions, terminating the conversation without saying good-bye. (One internal joke was that Greenberg conserved incremental bits of time through the course of his week by eliminating the small talk.) During the 1980s, when Cayne was still a stockbroker, he drove Greenberg to work every morning. Since the two men had little in common other than their employer, the rides were often spent in an uncomfortable silence.

Greenberg guarded fiercely against potential losses. His market-risk gatherings—called "cold sweat" meetings—were held every Monday afternoon at 4:10 P.M. and, with typical efficiency, lasted only twenty minutes. Most of the heavy lifting was done by a band of risk assessors known internally as "ferrets," who paced the trading desks throughout the week to look over employees' shoulders and see that the money at risk wasn't outsized. Because their role was to suss out dishonest behavior or problem trades before they cost Bear money, the ferrets took on a panoply of colorful nicknames: "the snoop," "the hawk," and "the weasel," among others.

During the meetings Greenberg would confront individual traders about their various positions, asking them to justify their strategies. One thing he looked for was "aged" holdings that had been on Bear's books for more than ninety days. Such positions, he often felt, were "stale," and needed to be moved out as soon as possible. In a 1993 article, Greenberg bragged about his airtight risk oversight to the *Wall Street Journal*. "The definition of a good trader is a guy who takes losses," he said. "The definition of an ex-trader is one who tries to cover up a loss." Get caught doing that, he added, and "you're out, O-U-T."

His basic mantra was straightforward: work hard, show commitment, and make big money. His hiring philosophy centered on the idea of recruiting a class of workers he called "PSDs": those who were poor, smart, and held a deep desire to be rich.

Starting late in 1978, he issued a series of memos to partners that gave directives on how to do business. Seemingly tongue-in-cheek, the missives nonetheless made his agenda clear. "We are working with more capital than ever before," he wrote in May 1980, "so if every month is not a record-breaker, we are probably getting lazy. We have plenty of room for improvement and there are still a number of leaks in the dike. In fact, the only area that I think is running at 100% efficiency is the error account." He added: "It is up to all of us to fight our unrelenting enemies—complacency, over-confidence and conceit."

He excoriated employees who left their desks for more than ten minutes without telling their secretaries where they could be reached. In June 1983 he issued the following warning: "I have contacted Marlin Perkins of the St. Louis Zoo and the next person that I have trouble finding will be fitted out with a radio collar. Please impress our policy on the people who work with and under you. The collars are bulky and not very attractive."

Expenses were another focal point. In an infamous 1985 message, sent not long before Bear sold its first shares to the public in an initial public offering of stock—a move that changed Greenberg's title from head partner to chief executive officer—he made a stern admonition: in order to keep spending down, Bear would cease to purchase paper clips. Employees were expected to reuse the paper clips they already had on hand, replenishing them only with ones taken from new documents they received during the day. He soon added interoffice envelopes to the list, but with a few instructions: Secretaries were to lick only the left side of the adhesive strip, so that if the envelopes were gently opened, they could be used in at least one future exchange by sealing only the right side. Rubber bands soon followed (if they broke, they were to be tied in a knot for future use).

To drive his points home, Greenberg created a fictitious business philosopher he named Haimchinkel Malintz Anaynikal, whom he liked to quote in the memos. In January 1984, he laid out his alter ego's key principles in another partner memo:

1. Stick to thine own business.
2. Watch thy shop.
3. Limit thy losses.
4. Watch thy expenses like a hawk.
5. Stay humble, humble, humble.
6. When dealing with a new account, know thy customer and know thy customer's money is up.

Part eccentric, part savant, Greenberg came to be widely respected on Wall Street. The firm's growth was impressive, and its culture was solid. Bear was a place where young, hungry workers could get a crack at the securities business and make big money if they played it smart. The firm even became known for hiring outcasts from other shops who were believed to be talented despite their missteps. In 1987, for instance, Howard Rubin was fired from Merrill Lynch after taking the fall for a $377 million loss. By 1993, his mortgage-bond group at Bear had made $150 million in profits and his take-home pay was $6.5 million.

Greenberg was tough, but he had a charitable spirit. In 1993, when an employee named Dennis Hom was hit by a car and died, Greenberg took up an internal collection to pay off the man's $181,000 mortgage so that his wife and children could stay in their home. He encouraged people to participate in charity raffles and events, including functions for the Boy Scouts and the United Jewish Appeal, some of which he hosted himself. Bear was also the only firm on the Street to employ a mandatory philanthropic giveback each year: Greenberg's mandatory charitable giving for SMDs was another source of pride. He liked to say that as much as his competitors seemed to admire the policy, not a single one ever adopted it themselves.

In 1993, after a protracted political fight with Cayne, Greenberg relinquished his job as CEO. But his influence continued. He remained chairman of the board and a member of the firm's executive committee, the powerful cabal of a half dozen executives who made all of Bear's major decisions. He continued running the cold-sweat meetings and kept his desk among those of the firm's stock traders. He was in daily contact with friends like Glickman, by then a Bear director, and continued advising clients like Donald Trump and Barbara Walters, whom he had dated in the early 1980s.

Greenberg's emphasis on spending curbs and on troubleshooting risks preserved the firm's reputation for watching its money. But Bear also had a knack for bending the rules to suit its needs. Not only did the firm hire traders who were considered black sheep by their former employers, it appeared to tolerate improper behavior for years at a time—only to tussle with regulators who then tried to cry foul.

In 1999, after a protracted legal process, the firm paid $35 million in fines and paybacks to investors—a huge sum at the time—to settle charges that it had overlooked signs of fraud at a boiler-room client for which it cleared. The client, a securities firm called A.R. Baron & Co., was accused of defrauding investors of $75 million by engaging in stock manipulation and other fraudulent activities. County prosecutors and SEC regulators argued that Bear's senior employees had turned a blind eye to the misconduct, and that the firm continued to clear trades for Baron as it ripped off unwitting customers. As a result, Richard Harriton, the head of Bear's clearing division, was personally fined and stripped of his job at the firm.

Like nearly all the major Wall Street firms, Bear also got caught up in the regulatory investigations of the early 2000s. It was part of the broad settlement made with New York Attorney General Eliot Spitzer in 2002, in which the investment banks paid some $1.4 billion to address charges that they issued boosterish research on shaky public companies in order to please their investment bankers, who were seeking deal fees for advising those companies. A swath of reforms followed. A couple of years later, however, Bear was again ensnared in questions about whether it skirted the law in an attempt to assist shady firm clients who were ripping off investors. In this case, the firm stood accused of helping trading clients who were engaging in improper "market timing," a kind of short-term trading that can lead to profits at the expense of long-term mutual-fund investors. Cayne was outraged by the accusations and vowed to fight the SEC. But the firm's protestations made little difference, and in 2006, Bear paid $250 million to settle the charges.

LATER SATURDAY
March 15, 2008

For three decades Jimmy Cayne had been an energetic, tough-talking culture carrier for Bear—the ultimate PSD.

He had grown up in Evanston, Illinois, a suburban enclave outside Chicago. His father was a patent lawyer. As a young man, Cayne had neatly coiffed dark hair and intense eyes. He attended Purdue University in West Lafayette, Indiana, about 150 miles east of Evanston. There he pledged the Sigma Alpha Mu fraternity, sang in the choir, and joined an air force training group and a campus Jewish organization. A semester before he was set to graduate in 1954, however, he dropped out and joined the army. In a 2008 interview with *Fortune*, he described himself as an indifferent student. "I hear and I absorb," he said, contrasting himself from his father, who was better at gathering book knowledge.

In the decade that followed, Cayne married, divorced, and moved to New York, where he restarted his life from scratch. In Chicago he had driven a cab and worked in his father-in-law's scrap-iron business as a salesman; in Manhattan, he did odd jobs to support his bridge habit. In 1971, he had a second marriage, to Patricia Denner, whom he had met at a card table.

Denner demanded he quit driving cabs and selling photocopiers and get a steadier job. So, two years before they married, Cayne found work as a junior broker at Bear. He used his bridge-world connections to network with potential clients, a tactic that helped him land his first big account with the media mogul Laurence Tisch, later the owner of the CBS network.

Cayne excelled in the big-money world of financial advising. He was an inveterate schmoozer whose entertaining yarns and salty language could make even high rollers feel at home. At Bear, then in its last few years under Cy Lewis's strict rule, he relished being one of the guys, cracking jokes around the office and comparing war stories from the business. His $70,000 starting salary soon ballooned.

In business, Cayne could be innovative. During New York City's financial crisis in 1975, when one of his clients was having trouble selling municipal bonds, the young broker offered to have Bear buy them and try to resell them on the open market—effectively creating a new secondary market for city bonds. Conservative-minded as always, Greenberg was opposed. So, in a calculated risk, Cayne went over his head and proposed the idea directly to Lewis. The head partner endorsed it, and a lucrative business was born.

It was one of many moments when Cayne felt that Greenberg lacked "balls," as he later told *Fortune*. He played bridge with Greenberg—the one interest, other than making money, that the two had in common—and continued driving him to work in the morning. But their discussions were painfully awkward, and a sense of kinship never ran deep.

Tisch and other important clients had solidified Cayne's reputation as a serious broker, and his political skills were soon driving him to the top of the firm. Along the way, he developed a knack for spotting talent in Bear's ranks—figures like Warren Spector and Jeff Mayer, who eventually became stars in the firm's fixed-income division, and Donald Tang, the Chinese-born investment banker who later helped ink Bear's partnership with CITIC.

By 1985, Cayne had been named the firm's president, and was running Bear's management and compensation committee. It was a far cry from his days as a starting broker, trying to impress his new girlfriend with his five-figure salary. By 1992, the year before he became CEO, Cayne's pay had swelled to $14.7 million—less than a million dollars shy of Greenberg himself. Bear executive compensation was so high, in fact, that it prompted the company to rein in the rules around executive bonuses. Just seven years into its tenure as a publicly traded company, the firm was garnering a reputation for overpaying its top brass—a remarkable feat for the smallest of the major investment banks.

By 1993, Cayne felt he was ready for the top job. He had long chafed under Greenberg's old-fashioned ways, and badly wanted a change.

The two men had different personalities and philosophies about how Bear should run. But they also maintained some petty rivalries. Cayne, for instance, couldn't stand that people referred to Greenberg, whose given name was Alan, as "Ace."* So Cayne's friends called the older man "Alan" anytime they were in Cayne's presence. Anyone who tripped up and called him "Ace" owed Cayne $100, as part of a longstanding bet.

Fortunately for Cayne, most of the company's leaders were in his back pocket by then. "He lost the ultimate power, I guess," Cayne told *Fortune* in 2008, reflecting on Greenberg's waning fan base at the time. "I had the executive committee and the board completely on my side." Moreover, by his own estimation, Cayne and those he oversaw were responsible for more than two-thirds of Bear's profits.

Cayne formed an alliance of directors and pushed Greenberg aside. Old-timers like Carl Glickman, a close friend of Greenberg's who had been on the Bear board since its IPO in 1985, were shocked. "When I first knew [Cayne], he was nothing," Glickman recalls. "He was a great salesman and an assistant to Ace. And he just kept coming up and coming up."

Greenberg, however, handled the coup with grace. Remaining on as chairman, he turned his day-to-day focus on trading for his own clients. Those who didn't know better would have said he and Cayne

---

*Greenberg's nickname, as he explained once to the television interviewer Charlie Rose, arose not from his successes as a young businessman but from his college years at the University of Missouri. Thinking a name like Alan Greenberg wouldn't help him win dates, a friend suggested he go by "Ace Gainsborough" instead. Though the last name got dropped, the first stayed with him.

were friends. Some likened them to an old married couple, who lived in a mutually understood symbiosis even though they couldn't stand each other's company.

The next ten years were good to both Bear and Cayne. Bond trading was exploding around the world, lifted by the growing prominence of emerging markets, the increased reliance on debt financing for corporate mergers and acquisitions, and a boom in commodities like oil. Housing prices in the United States enjoyed a multiyear run in which properties sold for more than they ever had in history, and packaging those loans into new securities became a lucrative niche. Bear's mortgage-origination, packaging, and trading businesses grew dramatically, and its investment-banking unit generated hefty fees, both from advising corporate clients and from helping them raise the debt capital they needed to do deals.

During Cayne's tenure, Bear's head count doubled to more than fourteen thousand employees, and it extended its operations into London and Asia. The stock price rose an eye-popping 600 percent. Profits grew, and Cayne managed to keep the firm's return on equity—an important measure of how much profit Bear churned out against the amount of capital its shareholders had invested—steady at about 15 percent. In 2003, Bear for the first time took in more than $1 billion in profits, and by 2006, its banner year, the figure was more than $2 billion.

Cayne's compensation kept pace with the company's rising fortunes. For the fiscal year 2006, he took home nearly $34 million in stock, options, pay, and bonus. (Schwartz and Spector, who earned $32 million apiece, weren't far behind.) His stock holdings, which amounted to more than 5 percent of Bear's total outstanding shares, were also lucrative. In the spring of 2006, with Bear shares topping the $140 mark, Cayne became the richest chief executive of a Wall Street firm in paper wealth, with shares valued at $1.02 billion. Of the other current and former heads of major financial firms, only former Citigroup chief Sanford Weill ran a close second, with holdings valued at $999 million. Cayne, emperor of the Street's most rough-edged firm, was the only paper billionaire.

As CEO, Cayne's style was to stay focused on the big picture and to manage the firm's labyrinthine internal politics. He did this by carefully controlling Bear's board and by handpicking mentees who would be forever loyal. He gathered information through casual lunches and one-on-one meetings in his office, where he'd quiz employees on the state of their businesses and what was going on with their superiors and coworkers. Once he had enough input, he'd decide privately on his next move.

Cayne adored his job, and he established a certain mystique. One rule of thumb was that he would not travel—even downtown—unless it was absolutely necessary. He detested being on the board of the New York Stock Exchange, because he disliked the journey from Madison Avenue to Wall Street, where the Big Board directors usually met. He famously told associates he wouldn't meet with President Bush to discuss economic matters unless the commander in chief traveled to Bear's offices himself.

A visit to Cayne's office, however, was well worth the trip. Once invited into his sleek, darkly lit suite, guests would be invited to smoke rare cigars, put their feet up, and chat about everything from politics (Cayne, an ardent Republican, had a particular dislike for Senator Hillary Clinton) to the growing international market for scrap metal (a commodity Cayne, who had once sold it, knew quite a bit about). He barked orders to his staff through a sliding partition to his right, beyond which his two longtime assistants, Charlotte and Suzette, manned his schedule and the phones. Charming and gregarious, Cayne left guests with the impression that he had nowhere else to be besides sitting there, shooting the breeze with them.

Lunch in one of Bear's private dining rooms was equally entertaining. Cayne would sit at the head of the table, brandishing the cigar he'd brought for after the meal, with little care for whether his guests minded the smoke or not. Picking at crudités, he'd tell amusing stories about friends like Ray Kelly, the New York City police commissioner, or the rash he'd gotten on his face after tasting a new breakfast cereal. A leather-bound menu offered an array of fresh catch, sandwiches, and pasta, served graciously by a waiter in formal attire.

Cayne viewed himself as indisputably in charge. "I'm going to be the last CEO of Bear Stearns," he would occasionally say, leaving companions to wonder what his plan was. Would he actually be willing to sell the company before passing it on to another executive? He had always said he'd do so only for an enormous premium on the company's stock price.

Many of Cayne's consiglieres worked in the company's powerful retail brokerage unit, known as private-client services. Even though PCS had a titular business head, Cayne personally oversaw his old division, and frequently palled around with its heaviest hitters. One of his closer friends was Kurt Butenhoff, the former Salomon Brothers broker whose clients included the Bahamanian billionaire Joseph Lewis. Late in the summer of 2007, when Lewis began loading up on Bear shares and became for a time the company's largest individual shareholder, Cayne's relationship with the elusive investor was given credit for bringing Lewis on board—even though SEC filings suggested that Lewis's stock purchases were actually the result of an options trade that had forced him to buy.

Outside the realms of PCS and stock trading, however, Cayne showed little aptitude. By 2001, the year Cayne became chairman, he was relying heavily on Spector and Schwartz, whom he had just named copresidents, to handle the firm's day-to-day operations. Spector alone had oversight of thousands of Bear's employees: Operations, stock and bond sales and trading, and asset management all reported to him. Schwartz oversaw the firm's investment-banking division, which numbered about one thousand employees. And he was plenty busy on the road, attending beauty contests for new advisory jobs and meeting with his existing clients.

Spector, whose businesses were ripe for growth, soon grew frustrated with Cayne's hesitancy to explore new areas. At a time when rivals like Goldman and Credit Suisse Group had made huge headway in China, for example, Bear had little or no presence in Asia, save for a handful of employees in Tokyo and Hong Kong. The expansion in London and into other areas, like asset management, were made over Cayne's initial objections. Handsome assets were for sale in the mutual-fund world, and yet he passed up a chance to buy the successful money manager Neuberger Berman, leaving Lehman Brothers to swoop in instead. Ironically, Cayne would later hire Neuberger's former head, Jeff Lane, to salvage his own flailing money manager, Bear Stearns Asset Management, after the two internal hedge funds blew up.

Those who sought Cayne's help with the more nitty-gritty aspects of Bear's business were often disappointed. During the early 2000s, Pat Lewis, then a midlevel employee in the firm's internal financial department, spent three years working on what he called the "risk-based capital allocation" plan, a way of assessing the financial health of Bear's various business units by seeing how much risk they took on relative to how much revenue they generated—in other words, their risk-adjusted returns. For three years Lewis and his boss tracked the numbers in Bear's key departments, and built the technical models needed to run the assessments. CFO Sam Molinaro liked the idea, and it seemed a sensible way to formulate decisions about the use of Bear's cash based on the soundness of the individual units it was supporting. All that was needed was a green light from Cayne.

Knowing their plan would require a bite-sized explanation, Lewis and his boss spent weeks working on what they called a "Jimmy document" that could explain how the risk-based capital allocation program would work in plain terms; the document was eventually presented to Cayne but it was all for naught. The CEO, who considered such matters to be strictly within Spector's purview, didn't understand how the plan would work, and dismissed it as being too complicated to bother with. Three years of effort were essentially wiped off the board.

Cayne paid far closer attention to the board of directors, of which he was made chairman in 2001. Over the years, Bear's board had included some industry titans, like the German-born entrepreneur John Kluge, who made a fortune in television, radio, and advertising in the 1960s, 1970s, and 1980s through his media company Metromedia, which he later sold to Rupert Murdoch, and Fred Wilpon, chief executive of the Mets baseball team. But the board also included a large number of firm associates and clients, some of whom had limited experience in investment banking and trading and were brought on board because of their friendships with key players.

One of those people was Carl Glickman. Born in 1926, he had earned his stripes as a real estate investor and owner of small businesses, splitting his time between his native Cleveland and New York, where he owned a string of apartments in some of the city's finest hotels. He had no hands-on experience as a stockbroker or trader, but Glickman did have a good understanding of business, and he had some friends in high places. Greenberg was one of them.

Glickman and Greenberg had met in the 1960s through a mutual acquaintance, and they became fast friends after that. Greenberg, always an active stock adviser to his list of personal clients, managed some investments for Glickman, and the two soon got in the habit of checking in by phone every day. Glickman, whose wife and children resided in the Cleveland suburbs, would spend time with Greenberg when he was in New York, where he spent half of his working hours. Eventually Glickman became an unofficial Bear employee, working out of Greenberg's conference room when he was in town and even having Greenberg's secretary answer his phone. (When Glickman was back in Ohio, she would patch calls that came into the Bear office to his office on Superior Avenue in downtown Cleveland.)

In addition to using Greenberg as an investment adviser, Glickman referred other business Bear's way, putting entrepreneur friends from the Midwest in touch with the firm's investment bankers when they wanted to go public. Between his real estate holdings and the small companies he owned, Glickman got around in the business world; at one point, he was on the board of sixteen different entities. So by the time Greenberg decided to take Bear public in 1985, his good friend and business associate was a shoo-in for the board.

Glickman made no bones about where his allegiances lay. "I was there because of Greenberg," he says. So when Cayne took over as board chairman in 2001—giving Greenberg yet another demotion—Glickman told his friend he wanted to resign. "If you're not here, I don't want to be here," he told Greenberg.

But Greenberg was steadfast. He planned to continue working with clients and maintain an active role in the company, where he was to chair the executive committee as well as run risk management. "I'm not leaving, and I want you to stay," he said. Glickman reluctantly agreed.

Things changed almost immediately after that. Board meetings were so scripted that the minutes were often written out in advance and directors were asked to read from prepared comments. "Jimmy called the shots," Glickman says. "It became a dictatorship as opposed to a corporation," he recalls.*

Shortly after Cayne took the chairman position, Glickman was removed from his longtime role as chairman of the audit committee. Two years later, when a raft of corporate-governance reforms were sparking many companies to name external board members to the

---

*Tese disagreed with this characterization on Cayne's behalf. "Jimmy always said to any member of the board, if you have any issue, say it," Tese said. "That was the culture of the company."

position of "lead" director to encourage more independent thinking, Glickman figured that as the nonmanagement director with the longest tenure at the company, he was the man for the job.

Over cigars one day, he decided to broach the topic with Cayne, who was distracted by a special blade Glickman was using to snip his cigar for flavor enhancement. "I want one of those," Cayne mused aloud.

"We've got to name a lead director," said Glickman. He, like many executives, had been watching the kerfuffle at the NYSE with a leery eye. Its chairman and CEO, Dick Grasso, was being raked over the coals by corporate-governance experts for packing his board with pals and beholden brokerage-industry leaders who had granted him nearly $200 million in compensation.

"Yes," Cayne replied.

"I think it's a job I could do," said Glickman.

"I've already picked someone," said Cayne. "Vincent Tese."

Tese had been on the board since 1994, the year after Cayne became CEO. Glickman was disappointed, but not surprised. Not long thereafter, to show there were no hard feelings, he presented Cayne with a gift: a cigar puncher of his own. But Cayne returned the gadget without explanation.

Henry Bienen, the respected president of Northwestern University, learned the hard way about Cayne's overweening influence. He joined the board in 2004 as one of its outside directors. Having never served on a public-company board before and lacking any formal background in finance, Bienen was initially impressed with the company's openness. As part of his own vetting process, he spent time with nominating committee head Fred Salerno at a diner near his Long Island home, discussing his new position. Then, after joining the board that fall, he spent two hours with Spector, discussing the firm's stock and bond businesses.

But Bienen, too, was disturbed by the perfunctory nature of Cayne's board meetings. So about a year into his tenure, he decided to speak up. Filling out an annual questionnaire about the effectiveness of Bear's board meetings, he wrote that while certain aspects of the board's operations seemed to be in good working order—audit committee meetings, for instance, tended to go on for hours—the full director meetings struck him as mere formalities, bereft of any serious discussion on strategy.

He was under the impression that the input in the questionnaires would remain anonymous—at least to Bear executives. But not long after he submitted his, he was called into Cayne's office for a talking-to that he later described to friends as a "woodshed" session.

"You don't understand the company," the CEO told Bienen, much to his surprise. Bear, said Cayne, required a "blocking and tackling" approach and was driven by minute-to-minute decisions on trading and other matters. There was no place, he added, for long-winded "strategy" sessions at the board level; rather, the key was to recruit good talent and remain nimble in fast-moving markets. Bienen got the message: Criticism was not welcome. After that, he kept his head down—even making a point of telling Tese that a second critical questionnaire that was filed the following year had not been his.

As a manager, Cayne was frequently absent. He built a vacation home near the New Jersey shore, and got in the habit of leaving work early on summer Thursdays to enjoy a long weekend there. In order to reach the local golf course before sundown, he ordered a helicopter service to take him from Manhattan to the Hollywood Golf Club in Deal, New Jersey, where he was a member.

Thursday evening's game was usually followed by another round on Friday morning. On the course, accompanied by friends like talk show host Maury Povich and hedge fund manager John Angelo, a Bear client, Cayne never brought a cell phone or a BlackBerry. If a crisis arose at Bear between breakfast and lunch, executives would have to call the club and hope to be patched in to a landline near one of the course's eighteen holes.

Cayne typically spent Saturdays and Sundays in Deal with his wife and extended family, which included his daughter and son-in-law, Alison and Jack Schneider, and a number of grandchildren. He played golf again on Saturday and Sunday mornings, and often returned to the house to play online bridge and poker afterward. Cayne was back in the office on Monday morning.

He also left town at least three times a year, sometimes more, to participate in the American Contract Bridge League's North American Bridge Championship games, which were held in March, July, and November. The tournaments, held in a rotating series of domestic cities, usually at midtier hotels, lasted for ten days, and Cayne and his wife typically attended for the duration. Games would be played throughout the afternoons and evenings, leaving little time to check in with the office. During the winter holiday season, he often flew to Florida for a couple of weeks to wind down and ring in the new year.

Molinaro, Schwartz, and Spector had by then grown used to Cayne's absenteeism and lack of interest in details. Spector, in fact, eventually began to emulate him. Soon after purchasing a vacation home in the Chilmark section of Martha's Vineyard in 1996, he and his wife, the actress Margaret Whitton, began leaving on Thursdays or Fridays during the summer to spend long weekends there. Spector also attended some of the same bridge tournaments the Caynes did. Cayne was ensconced at the company, the trio felt, and Bear's performance was just fine—better than fine. No one ever gave serious thought to the idea of unseating Cayne before he was good and ready. Even if they had, the board was still well within his control.

But Cayne had another habit that would soon cause the firm embarrassment: He liked to smoke marijuana. This pastime was well known to some close associates, who had seen him smoking in his Park Avenue apartment. It had also come to the attention of some of the regulars on the bridge circuit, where Cayne was known to retire to his room after the day's play and tuck into his pot stash as a way to relax.

Roy Welland, an options trader, Bear client, and tournament regular, still remembers a particular run-in he had with Cayne during the Boston championships in November 1999. On the night Welland and his family arrived at the hotel, their room hadn't been ready, so they were put in a bedroom in the presidential suite, whose occupants had not yet arrived.

The following morning, Welland's two-year-old twin boys were still asleep when the hotel management called to say that the presidential suite's expected guests had arrived and that the family would have to clear out. But Welland's reserved room still wasn't ready, and after a long evening of travel, he didn't want to wake the sleeping boys. Still, the hotel was insistent, and security was soon banging on the door, asking the family to leave.

While Welland was arguing with the hotel staff, he and his wife noticed a funny smell seeping under the door of his room: pot smoke. Outraged by the hotel's harassment and the fact that his neighbors were using illegal drugs so obviously that his toddlers might notice it, Welland says he called the Boston police, who sent an officer over to interview them. Afterward, when the Wellands finally left their room to move into the one they had reserved, they saw Cayne's bridge partner standing in the hall in his underwear, surrounded by a cloud of pot smoke, and heard the unmistakable voices of Jimmy and Patricia Cayne coming from within the room. Cayne, through representatives, denies the incident. Boston police department records reflect that officers responded to a call from a Roy Welland staying at the Westin Hotel during that time period, but do not mention either Cayne or a marijuana smell. Hotel management declined comment.

Five years later, Cayne's marijuana use was discovered by another bridge-circuit regular at a Memphis Doubletree. After the day's competition, he invited a fellow player and a woman to join him for a smoke in a lobby men's room. The player declined, but the woman followed him in and shared a joint with Cayne, to the amusement of a third party, who was finishing up in the men's room when they arrived. Cayne and the woman were standing just inside the doorway, near the sinks. In November 2007, the Memphis story was disclosed in a front-page article about Cayne in the *Journal,* though Cayne denied the incident. He later told *Fortune,* "There is no chance that it happened," he said. "Zero chance." But when asked about his pot use generally, he refused to answer, saying he would respond only "to a specific allegation."

For years, these situations remained mostly under wraps, as Bear and its CEO remained feared and admired. But as the housing boom showed its first signs of strain, Cayne's foibles seemed less amusing.

In January 2007, Bear shares hit their all-time high of $172. The issuance of new mortgages was at record levels, and the lucrative securitization business was booming. At the same time, Bear was exploring new business arenas—albeit a bit later than many of its rivals. It was expanding Bear Stearns Asset Management, which had recruited top players from both within and outside the firm, was branching into the growing energy-trading business, and was building a new European headquarters in London's Canary Wharf. The firm's respected credit analyst remained bullish on the housing sector, and Bear seemed positioned for another standout year.

But within weeks, the mortgage market had its first major hiccup. Securities backed by mortgages that had been issued to subprime borrowers, or those with patchy credit histories, began to crater. Housing prices around the United States, buoyant just a few months ago, began to fall. The packaging of mortgage loans into new securities slowed as a result, forcing firms like Bear and even Goldman to cancel new product offerings that had been months in the planning and face sudden holes in their revenue estimates.

Then Bear's two hedge funds fell apart. Starting in June, when news of investors requesting their money back first hit the trade magazines, the implosion of the High-Grade Structured Credit Strategies Fund and its more leveraged sister fund played out in ghastly form on the pages of the *Journal*, Bloomberg, and other financial outlets.

Late that June, Cayne gave an interview to the *New York Times* about the company's predicament. "I'm angry," he said, puffing on a Montecristo cigar. "When you walk around with a reputation for being the most rigorous risk analyzer, assessor, controller, and that is trashed, well, you have got to feel bad. This is personal." It was, he said, "a body blow of massive proportion."

It wasn't enough of a blow to keep him in the office, however. During July, after the funds had received the $1.6 billion bailout from their parent company (the full $3.2 billion hadn't been needed), and Marano, who had left his day job on the seventh floor, had transferred to BSAM to help clean up the mess, Cayne continued with his golf outings and a long-planned stint at a bridge tournament in Nashville. The funds soon filed for bankruptcy protection.

When Cayne returned, the firm was in tumult. Lenders were showing signs of leeriness toward funding Bear, and were demanding far stiffer terms to do so. The company's stock had been tumbling, and regulators and potential suitors were circling.

On Wednesday, August 1, Cayne called Spector into his office.

Cayne was sitting behind his desk, and Spector settled into a chair across from him. He didn't know what was coming, but he knew it wasn't going to be anything good. Cayne had been cold to his former protégé ever since he returned from the tournament.

"I can't work with you anymore," Cayne finally said.

Spector wanted to know why. "Let's go through it," he said.

"No," said Cayne. "I don't want to discuss it." He looked pained. "I have to show leadership," he said. "Something has to be done. I can't work with you anymore, so you have to go."*

---

*A representative for Cayne says his recollection is that the August 1 meeting with Spector was preceded by a discussion with members of the board's audit committee, who agreed that Spector should be asked to leave.

Spector, who had brought a pen and paper with him, was taking notes. Cayne seemed uncomfortable. "What are you doing?" he asked Spector.

"I don't want to get this wrong," Spector said, "so I'm taking notes."

Cayne was silent.

Spector tried to argue. His departure wouldn't be good for the firm, he told Cayne. It had already been a crushingly busy year, and now Bear was in crisis over the fallen hedge funds. But Cayne wanted no further discussion. He ended the meeting after five minutes.

In fact, Cayne had a litany of complaints about the way his underling had handled the BSAM mess. Among other things, Cayne was irate that Spector had personally authorized a $25 million infusion into the funds as they were swirling down the drain, without checking with anyone. The firm now had some $45 million invested in a dud, not just the $20 million it had started out with. And that was only the latest infraction.

Word of Cayne's demand got around quickly after that. Molinaro and Schwartz were opposed to the move, and warned Cayne about their concerns. Despite his flaws, Spector had a strong handle on the firm's most important businesses, they argued. They needed him at this troubled time in the mortgage market; it was a bad time to let him go. But Cayne was adamant. He felt Spector had humiliated the firm and had to leave.

A couple of days later, Spector and Whitton left for their home on Martha's Vineyard. He had decided to quit. All that was left was the decisive board meeting, then scheduled for Monday.

On Friday, August 3, Bear's stock took a beating. Despite efforts by Upton and Molinaro to assure investors that the firm's funding was secure, Bear shares hit a new twelve-month low of less than $107. Word of Spector's ouster leaked out after the close of trading on Friday, adding to the anxiety of Bear's future. Over the weekend, firm managers were forced to sit down with overseers from the SEC and a due-diligence team from Kohlberg Kravis Roberts & Co. Suddenly Bear was in play.

Cayne moved the board meeting about Spector's resignation up to Sunday, hoping to get the official news out well before Monday's opening bell. His exit was approved. To celebrate that night, Cayne and Tese went out for Chinese food with Charlie Gasparino, a CNBC reporter with whom Cayne had long been chummy. Cayne expressed his optimism about Bear's future, and told Gasparino he had scheduled a meeting for the following day with executives from Citigroup, one of Bear's biggest lenders, to discuss the funding picture. Gasparino reported the news the next morning.

The meeting at Citi ultimately led to nothing, and Bear's executives spent the next few weeks scrambling for solutions. To meet the most immediate capital needs, the firm raised $2.25 billion in a public bond offering, paying an unusually high fee to do so. But executives were uncertain how to rebuild longer-term confidence. Schwartz, who had convinced the Kohlberg team to come in, thought a strategic investor might help burnish Bear's image, and began pursuing other suitors. Later that month, a team from J.C. Flowers stopped in; executives also held talks with PIMCO. But the idea Cayne and Schwartz most warmed to was that of a strategic tie-up with CITIC, the Chinese investment bank, which would give Bear a better foothold in Asia and provide a $1 billion capital infusion within a few months. Over Labor Day weekend, Cayne made a rare trip overseas for business, flying to Beijing to help make the deal. By late October, Bear and CITIC had an agreement in principle.

It would be Cayne's last major accomplishment as CEO. Through September, he had battled a life-threatening blood infection and had nearly died at the hospital. After a catheterization and several weeks' rest, he returned to the office, looking pale and wan. Cayne, whose swept-back white hair usually contrasted nicely with his deep tan, had already lost twenty pounds that year as part of a no-red-meat diet, and now, his sickly demeanor and additional weight loss made him look practically ghostly.

The November 1 pot-smoking story in the *Journal* didn't help. Suddenly Bear's rank and file, who had long found Cayne a lovable eccentric, were no longer amused. And the firm was headed for its first-ever quarterly loss, and its biggest liability seemed to be its CEO.

By late December, major shareholders were calling the board to push for Cayne's ouster. Word began circling back to him. Knowing he was under pressure, he informed the outside directors of his thoughts of retirement, then went to Boca Raton for the holidays.

On January 8, when Cayne was named nonexecutive chairman, he was removed from the payroll and even lost his medical benefits. "I don't deserve them," he told Tese in a moment of humility. It was a huge comedown for the once-mighty CEO.

As chairman, Cayne rarely came into the office, monitoring things from home instead. He and Patricia were in the process of buying a $26 million pair of apartments in the former Plaza Hotel on Central Park South, and he was still regaining his health.

The board, however, continued functioning under Cayne's special brand of politics, and Henry Bienen soon became the newest castoff. On the day Schwartz's promotion to CEO was announced, Bienen decided, after a long silence as a Bear director, to grant a handful of short media interviews about the transition. Though complimentary about Schwartz and about Bear in general, he took issue with Cayne's absence during the hedge fund crisis. "Being absent at a time of crisis is not a good thing," Bienen told the *Journal*, adding that "at a time when things are going very haywire in the credit markets . . . it's really important to be seen."

Shortly after that, Bienen was informed by fellow director Fred Salerno that he would probably not be standing for reelection to the board at Bear's annual meeting that April. Bear already had one educator, St. John's University's Father Donald Harrington, on the board, and there was a desire to bring on some fresh blood from the securities industry, Salerno explained. Though he had been a director for only a short time, Bienen agreed. But to associates he wondered aloud whether the move was retribution for crossing some invisible line.

1:00 P.M.

The full board gathered for another call around 1:00 on Saturday afternoon. Tese and Salerno, en route to 383 from John F. Kennedy International Airport, participated from a taxicab. Tese was somewhat relieved to have brought Rodge Cohen on board to advise the nonmanagement directors. He had also decided to follow every full board meeting with a separate gathering of the nonmanagement board members, to make sure everyone's interests were aligned.

Still, there was little news to report as yet. Schwartz brought the group up to date on the goings-on so far that day, and told those who hadn't yet heard that Bear was down to two days for negotiating, rather than twenty-eight. The board wouldn't know much more until a hard bid emerged from either J.P. Morgan or, God willing, some other party.

David Kim, the derivatives contract lawyer, had worked all night on Friday, arriving home to Summit just before midnight. On Saturday, he got another call from his boss, asking if he could come in. Kim said no; he and his wife had guests over. But he agreed to pitch in from home.

He retreated to the master bedroom with his laptop, and spent the afternoon on the phone with colleagues. It was tedious work. His children, four-year-old Ryan and two-year-old Megan, kept wanting to come in. "Daddy can't talk right now," he kept telling them, feeling guilty for leaving his wife alone with their friends. Outside, the Kims' friends put their own hamburgers on the grill.

2:00 P.M.

Over at 383, bad news continued trickling in. At 2:09 that afternoon, a disturbing e-mail hit the in-boxes of a number of mortgage traders on the seventh floor.

Forwarded by someone at the mortgage originator First Franklin, the note was written by someone at Countrywide Financial, the large home-loan provider in Southern California. A huge originator of home loans, Countrywide claimed to account for some 16 percent of new U.S. mortgages at one point during the housing boom. It also stood accused of operating under shoddy standards and of not performing the proper diligence on borrowers, helping fuel the skepticism that now pervaded the debt markets as mortgage holders defaulted in increasing numbers.

The note was entitled "Bear Stearns Trades." It was remarkable for the chipper way in which it relayed a devastating proclamation:

"Currently Countrywide Home Loans is not accepting Bear Stearns trades. Please feel free to contact if you have any questions. Thank you!" The name of the sender had been cut off.

When Tom Marano read the e-mail, his response was strong: *"I will get somebody assigned to this asap."* He wanted to know who had decided that Countrywide wouldn't trade with Bear and for what reason.* This sort of missive could have a domino effect, as other

*Spokespeople for Countrywide, now a unit of Bank America Corp., did not respond to requests for comment.

firms got wind of the fact that one of their peers refused to trade with Bear. Within hours or days, Bear could be faced with a sea of competitors who refused to engage in any transactions, grinding its business to a halt.

Down on the fourth floor, the equities heads were thinking about their futures. Sitting in a conference room near Steve Meyer's office, Meyer, Lisman, his older cochief of equities, Jeremy Hill, who handled the division's financing, and several others had been discussing the day's events. They had met with J.P. Morgan. The group wondered if that would be it. Where were the other suitors who would help Bear spur a real bidding war? Surely they couldn't be held hostage by just one potential buyer.

Like many of their coworkers in other divisions, however, the stock traders were no longer shocked, just anxious. Since the funding crisis that had followed the hedge fund meltdowns last August, Meyer and Lisman had been expecting an even bigger crisis to envelop Bear. They knew now that time was of the essence. If anything, Friday's Fed loan had sped up the pullout of client funds, not reversed it. Monday would be mayhem if Bear opened for business without a partner.

The group had been checking the Bloomberg wire throughout the afternoon. Speculation outside 383 was also rife. Bear's equities team had heard some of the same rumors now being reported: that HSBC, the large British bank, might be interested; and that Barclays Bank, one of HSBC's competitors, was also in the mix. They had been asked earlier that day to stand by for more due-diligence meetings with another, unnamed party later that afternoon. Munching on sandwiches and worrying about their portfolios, the group waited for more information.

At 2:56, an answer of sorts came through. It was an e-mail from Steve Begleiter. "All, I apologize," he wrote, "but the other party just called and will not be coming in."

3:00 P.M.

Three stories above, Paul Friedman was again e-mailing with his pal at Barclays. "Get any rest?" the friend wrote.

"I'm in the office giving the place to JPM. If they'l[l] take it," Friedman replied about 3:20.

"I hope the fed is giving u an assist," the friend replied. "Heard Barclays might b[e] talking as well. Any truth to that?"

"Fed is clueless—worried but clueless," Friedman wrote. "Our CEO spoke to yours but I don't think there was much interest."

A little while later, he heard from Susie, at home in Scarsdale. "Bloomberg reports RBS is interested in buying you guys," she wrote, referring to the Royal Bank of Scotland, whose Greenwich Capital group was supposedly looking to grow its mortgage-trading operations.

"Close," Friedman answered. "RBC (Royal bank of Canada), not RBS . . . likes us a lot but there are lots of issues and little time."

It was several hours before Paulson could track down Josef Ackermann, Deutsche's chairman. The Treasury secretary asked him point-blank if he was serious about considering an overture.

"Not only are we not serious, but if those guys go down, we're not interested in doing business with any bank in the United States," Ackermann told him. Ackermann says through a spokesman that he told Paulson he might be interested in purchasing parts of Bear, but not the whole, and that he expressed to Paulson "grave worries" about the "legal risks" of such a deal.

Either way it was a shocking statement coming from one of the biggest foreign banks—to the top economic official in the administration, no less. Paulson was taken aback. "I realize we need to come up with a solution here," he said. But Ackermann's position, he added, did not show a very constructive attitude.

So Deutsche Bank was scratched off the list.

Back at 383, Gary Parr was working all angles. If Bear couldn't find a buyer for its entire business, he reasoned, maybe it could sell some prime assets off in chunks. At least that would raise some capital and preserve some jobs, possibly giving the firm a little more time to stave off bankruptcy.

The prime-brokerage unit, he knew, was Bear's ace in the hole. Since late the previous year, Parr had been talking on and off to Middle Eastern investors about the possibility of extending Bear's hedge fund client services into their region. Sovereign wealth was exploding in the oil-rich countries, and Bear had no footprint there; a strategic tie-up that brought Bear's expertise in the trading business to foreign investors and their cash, in turn, to Bear had seemed at the time like a great idea. Now, of course, things were far more desperate.

Parr dialed John Mack, the CEO of Morgan Stanley, where he had once worked as a senior investment banker. He explained what he was dealing with, and asked Mack if his firm would be interested in buying Bear's prime-brokerage business to augment its own.

"This is serious," Parr told him. "We're not wasting your time. Something's going to happen."

Mack said he would think about it. He was surrounded by his senior management that weekend, he explained, and would have an opportunity to ask them what they thought. If they were on board, he could probably send a team to 383 to review Bear's businesses quickly.

Bob Upton spent much of the afternoon in his sixth-floor office, preparing a calendar of Bear's funding for the month to come. He was enormously drained. After years of dressing smartly for the office in a suit and tie, he had shown up in casual pants and a button-down shirt that day. It felt to him like a small act of defiance. He'd always figured that if you wanted to be an important executive, you had to dress the part. But he was so anxious and sleep-deprived after the past few days, his outfit hardly seemed to matter.

News of the two-day deadline had not yet been widely disseminated, and Upton was still laboring under the assumption that they might be alive for another twenty-eight days as a stand-alone entity. Therefore, Bear needed an accounting of what debts were coming due on which days in the coming weeks.

Joining Upton was Pat Lewis, his deputy and good friend. Lewis was focused on the job, but didn't seem to have his heart in it. The professional number cruncher, who had long been frustrated by the dynamics at Bear, had in fact been interviewing for a job at UBS, the large Swiss investment bank, for a similar job in finance. Bear's worsening straits that weekend were only amplifying his desire to get out the door after such a long and painful slog.

Bear's financing picture at that point was nothing short of terrifying. The firm was in relatively solid standing on the equities side, where only a few billion of a total of tens of billions of dollars in funding were set to be refreshed on Monday. But on the fixed-income side, the number was more intimidating. A good deal of the funding was due to roll on Monday, and in a worst-case scenario, Bear could be looking at a need to raise up to $50 billion.

Upton and Lewis wondered what would happen with J.P. Morgan. Would the bank be willing to somehow guarantee Bear's trades as it went into the following week? In other words, would it tell lenders and clients that even if Bear were to run out of money, J.P. Morgan would be good for it? Only with such an assurance, it seemed to the treasurers, would Bear be able to move forward for business on Monday.

5:30 P.M.

Chris Flowers had spent most of his day on the phone. He and his team had made themselves at home in Cayne's spacious suite. It was surreal. In what other situation would potential buyers have free rein over the company chairman's office while he was still running the board? But Cayne had not yet shown up, and space was by now at a premium at 383, where lawyers, traders, bankers, and suitors were spilling out of every conference room on the sixth, twelfth, thirteenth, and forty-second floors.

In talking with investors, Flowers had a set speech. "We're trying to raise some financing," he'd say, "and we need to do it right now." Bear was clearly in trouble, he'd explain, and J.C. Flowers was interested in putting together a consortium of investors to help it out.

Flowers had spoken to senior people at General Electric's GE Capital Division, the TD Bank Financial Group in Toronto, Goldman, and Harvard University's endowment, among others. Most balked at the short time frame, as they had earlier in the day with Parr, arguing that such a complex company with such deep problems would require more than thirty-six hours of due diligence for any buyer. The exception was GE, which was interested in a secured investment of multiple billions of dollars. The Flowers team was pleased. GE had a reputation for being plodding and indecisive with investments, but here they were offering a pleasant surprise.

But by far the most memorable call took place around 5:30, when he drew a deep breath and called Warren Buffett's office in Omaha, Nebraska.

Flowers was unsure how Buffett would respond. Ever since his troubled investment in Salomon Brothers, the trading unit that had eventually been absorbed by Citigroup, the Omaha investor had largely steered clear of trading shops and investment banks, sticking to other businesses, like newspapers, candy, and insurance, to fill out Berkshire Hathaway's enormously successful portfolio of companies.*

Buffett had taken a controlling stake in Salomon Brothers in 1987, at a time when it was fending off a hostile offer from the corporate raider Ronald Perelman. The company had proved, however, to be a huge headache—even for one of American's savviest investors. A top player in the trading of mortgage-backed securities and other fixed-income products, Salomon was dominated by an unruly collection of well-compensated traders who engaged in high-stakes poker games, among other shenanigans, on the trading floor. The team was almost unaffordable in good times, but when a group of Salomon's best players left to open Long-Term Capital Management in the early 1990s, the gap had been exceedingly hard to fill. Salomon's attempts to build a first-rate investment bank to compete with rivals like Goldman and Morgan had flailed. And since a 1991 scandal involving a false bid in an auction of Treasury bonds, Salomon had carried a whiff of impropriety. It came as a great relief to Buffett in 1997, when he was finally able to offload the company to Citi's Sandy Weill.

Still, Buffett maintained close ties to Wall Street, as a client to many firms and as a personal friend of some executives. One of his buddies over the years had been Ace Greenberg. Buffett and Greenberg, just three years apart in age, were fellow Midwesterners who shared a love of bridge and a flair for sarcasm.† In 1996, when Green-

---

*In the fall of 2008, Buffett would make his first big exception, investing $5 billion in Goldman Sachs, then struggling with its own plummeting stock price and lack of market confidence.

†For a brief period in the late 1980s, Buffett and Greenberg had played together on a competitive bridge team they nicknamed CASH, for "Corporate America's Six Honchos." At various points the team included Cayne, the publishing magnate Malcolm Forbes, the Cravath, Swaine & Moore trust lawyer George Gillespie, and philanthropist Milton Petrie. CASH's final game was played at Forbes's U.K. residence late in February 1990, just days before Forbes died.

berg's partner memos had been published in a book called *Memos from the Chairman*, Buffett had penned an admiring but tongue-in-cheek introduction about Greenberg and his firm:

"Ace Greenberg does almost everything better than I do," wrote Buffett, "bridge, magic tricks, dog training, arbitrage—all the important things in life. He so excels at these that you might think it would give deep inferiority complexes to his colleagues at Bear Stearns. But if you think that, you don't know much about his colleagues."

Sitting in his Omaha office, Buffett picked up the phone, to Flowers's surprise. "I'm calling about Bear Stearns," Flowers began. "Should I go on?"

Buffett almost had to chuckle. It was sort of like having a woman standing in front of you who had taken half her clothes off and then asked whether she should continue, he thought. Just as he'd want the woman to finish the job, he was certainly curious to hear what was happening that weekend with the embattled Bear. He told Flowers to continue.

Buffett talked the idea through. "It has to look like you're doing the world a favor if you do this deal," he told Flowers. Flowers understood what he meant. A price of $2 to $3 per share would be devastating for Bear Stearns shareholders, whose stock had been trading at $30 only a day ago and $60 the day before. In order for the deal to fly, it would have to appear as though the buyers had helped stave off financial Armageddon, helping millions of investors and other companies in the process. You didn't want to look like a bunch of vultures coming in to gobble it up.

But Buffett himself was not interested. "It's not my favorite industry," he said of the brokerage business. "I learned my lesson with Salomon Brothers."

He paused for a second, then threw out a sardonic challenge. "You know what?" he said. "If Ace Greenberg is putting his money in there, I'll put my money in under the same terms that Ace Green-berg is." With that, he ended the call. Flowers and his team crossed Buffett off their list.

Gary Parr was increasingly worried about Schwartz. The CEO had been working nonstop since Thursday morning, after rushing back from Palm Beach, where he'd pressed the flesh all week with inves-tors and clients. Despite his youthful demeanor, which made him look younger than his fifty-seven years, the week's strains were start-ing to show on Schwartz's face.

Parr had been through many deals in his career, and had devel-oped a rule of thumb he liked to share with the younger bankers on his team: Sleep, eat, and use the bathroom whenever possible. There's no point in waiting around between meetings or calls and passing out because you're so hungry. Deals were often a long game, he felt, and he couldn't lose his key players before halftime.

Early in the evening, Parr spotted Schwartz in a sixth-floor cor-ridor and pulled him aside. "You've got to go take a nap," he said. "You've got to be rested. You've got a lot to go." Bear staffers were hard at work on the due-diligence materials that suitors needed, he explained. It was a good time to take a break.

Schwartz demurred. "I need to be here," he said. "I want to be here. Everybody's working hard, and nobody's getting a lot of rest."

6:00 P.M.

Sam Molinaro was sitting with Schwartz in his office late that after-noon when Steve Black called. After reviewing Bear's books that day, J.P. Morgan executives felt there might be a deal to be done, Black said.

That was the good news. The bad news was that the price range under consideration was quite low. The bank was considering a bid of between $8 and $12 per share. Even that spectrum was tentative, Black explained, because the J.P. Morgan teams still hadn't fully vetted the mortgage portfolio. His people had asked for additional files and information on positions, Black said, and would require the full night to review them. He'd be back in touch in the morning.

The Bear executives were cordial on the phone. Privately, however, they were flabbergasted. Molinaro in particular couldn't believe the position they were in. Schwartz never had a chance to negotiate, he realized. Bear had so little leverage that its CEO could not tell J.P. Morgan that their lowball bid—literally a third of where the stock had traded on Friday!—was unacceptable.

He and Schwartz talked it over. Could they rebuff J.P. Morgan? Molinaro asked. No matter how he looked at it, Bear was worth more than $8 to $12 per share. Just yesterday, Schwartz and Molinaro had told analysts on the investor call that Bear's book value—the value the company assigned itself per share—was still intact, at more than $80 per share. Even with a substantial discount, Bear was worth at least $50 to $60 per share—wasn't it?

Away from the raw numbers, there was also the consideration of how J.P. Morgan could run a company if most of its employees simply fled. Sure, some Bear workers would lose their jobs in an acquisition, but what about the better-paid managers and executives who had much of the expertise? If their stock holdings were wiped out in a takeover done at a basement price, perhaps they would quit out of sheer pique—that is, after they had stuck around long enough to try to vote down the deal.

Slowly Molinaro realized that they couldn't play hardball. They simply had no bargaining power. Bear was facing a bad deal, it seemed, or bankruptcy. In a bankruptcy situation, angry managers would become a moot point. The company's doors would be padlocked, paychecks and benefits would be immediately halted, and many of Bear's assets would be seized. He and Schwartz had no choice but to stick it out with J.P. Morgan.

Schwartz began making the rounds, letting those still in the building know where they stood. Marano was nearby, meeting with Jeff Mayer and Craig Overlander, the two heads of Bear's fixed-income division, when the CEO popped his head in.

"I think I've got them at eight to twelve dollars," Schwartz said, as if to put a positive spin on the situation.

Marano had almost ceased to care at that point. "Great," he replied, "go for it. But try to get higher."

Paul Friedman was in the CFO's conference room when Schwartz walked by. He, Begleiter, and a couple of other staffers were picking through the scraps of the last few days, looking for something to eat. It was an unappetizing spread. Soggy pizza and leftover Chinese food were laid out next to warm soda cans and cold coffee. Napkins and plastic utensils were scattered throughout the room. The trash hadn't been removed in nearly two days, and the smell of aging, greasy food filled the air.

Schwartz told the group about the call he'd just gotten from Black. "Confidentially, they're going to make us a bid, somewhere between eight and twelve dollars," he said. "They're going to their board Sunday morning."

Low as the price was, the group was relieved. It sounded like something would get done to save the firm from bankruptcy. What that meant for their stock holdings hadn't yet sunk in.

6:30 P.M.

Jimmy Cayne arrived shortly before 7:00 to find Schwartz, Molinaro, Tese, and Nick Nickell, the Bear director and fellow bridge player who ran the small brokerage Kelso & Company, discussing the bid in Molinaro's conference room. The atmosphere was funereal. Cayne asked what was going on.

Schwartz briefed the chairman on the call from Black and the price range J.P. Morgan was toying with. Cayne appeared stunned. "Well, eight to twelve dollars doesn't mean twelve, it means eight bucks," he said. Even at such distressed levels, the closing price Friday had been thirty dollars, he noted. "Why would we do it at eight? This firm is worth more if we took our chances with bankruptcy."

The executives and directors disagreed, trying to explain that a bankruptcy filing would be devastating for Bear and its employees. But Cayne seemed unconvinced.

Moments later, Schwartz convened a board call to tell the directors who weren't in the building about the possible deal with J.P. Morgan. "They're still doing their due diligence," he explained. "We've been given certain assurances, but there are hooks on those assurances."

By "hooks," Schwartz meant questions about the quality of Bear's assets. In other words, J.P. Morgan was still running Bear's positions through its own risk models, and unless the bank could be satisfied that the positions were relatively safe, there were no guarantees.

J.C. Flowers was also in the game, Schwartz added, but their prospects didn't seem good. The private-equity firm would require the backing of one or more large commercial banks, as well as the blessing of the Fed. Still, Bear would do all it could to encourage Flowers, he said, since a two-party bidding process was far preferable to the alternative.

Schwartz took some questions. Directors wanted to know the likelihood of the J.P. Morgan deal. Schwartz and Molinaro were encouraged, if not by the price, then by the tentative offer, and they were awaiting deal papers that night. But it was impossible to say whether the pact would be approved at that point. Dimon needed the approval of his board, among other things.

Bear's lawyers, who had spent most of their day convening in and around Schwartz's office on the forty-second floor, spent the night waiting for deal papers from J.P. Morgan to come through. Molinaro, who had spent much of the afternoon helping Upton prepare an accounting of how much funding Bear would need each day for the next month, lingered, too.

8:00 P.M.

By dinnertime, Flowers had their term sheet prepared. The firm hadn't come up with the $20 billion it had hoped for, but it was ready to invest $3 billion of its own capital and additional billions from GE. Moreover, the Flowers group had come up with an elegant way to handle some of Bear's riskier mortgage assets. It would create a new security to hold the troubled loans and leases and try to attract new investors who might be interested in distressed debt—in this case, mortgages that would eventually rise in value but could be had right now on the cheap.

It had been a very long two days for the Flowers team, part of which had arrived late morning on Friday and been camping out since then. Accompanying Chris Flowers was a handful of fellow Goldman alums: Jacob Goldfield, a former Harvard physics student and accomplished derivatives trader who had once chaired the firm's risk committee; John Oros, a financial-institutions banker who had worked alongside Flowers at the firm; and Mark Winkelman, who had run the firm's fixed-income unit and had worked closely with Lloyd Blankfein, later Goldman's CEO, at its commodities-trading unit, J. Aron & Co. The group's effort to buy Bear, however, had not been without levity. Flowers was somewhat chagrined that night when Cayne, who had arrived on the scene for the first time all weekend, popped into his own office to find the buyout team spread out with their feet up on his coffee table.

"I'm using my bathroom," Cayne told the group. "Help yourself," one of them replied. "We've been using it all weekend." Cayne looked uncomfortable.

For much of the day, Flowers had tried to convince Alan Schwartz that Goldman ought to be invited in. Whatever feelings they had about their alma mater, the J.C. Flowers team knew Goldman would be both savvy and fast-moving in the right kind of deal. Bear needed to stabilize the situation in its prime-brokerage division, where clients were exiting fast, and Goldman might be a willing buyer. Why not give them a call?

Schwartz, like other Bear executives, appeared uneasy. Goldman was one of Bear's top competitors, and its senior people had a reputation for being arrogant and demanding when it came to dealing with troubled target companies. Schwartz wasn't convinced that Goldman had an interest in buying Bear, and the only thing he'd heard they were interested in—the commodities unit—wasn't an asset he particularly wanted to sell. Bear's managers, who were working like dogs on the J.P. Morgan and Flowers due diligence, were already stretched thin. Schwartz worried that if Goldman showed up, it would stretch his team even thinner, without accomplishing much of anything.

But by Saturday night, perhaps encouraged by the tentative J.P. Morgan bid, Schwartz had softened. Tell Goldman it's all right to come over, he told Flowers.

A little while later, Goldfield, who had left 383 to attend a dinner, got an e-mail from Blankfein himself. The Goldman chief was aware of Bear's situation and was interested in hearing more about how his firm might get involved. Goldfield e-mailed Blankfein back with Mark Winkelman's number, explaining that he was still on the scene.

The Flowers bid was predicated on some significant help from the Fed. Together with staffers from Geithner's office, Flowers had worked out a proposal in which it would borrow, just like commercial banks, from the discount window—an unheard-of option for investment banks and buyout firms—in order to restore market confidence that Bear wouldn't run out of funding if the bank run continued. Flowers was also proposing a short grace period for the newly packaged distressed debt security in order to have the new security assessed by rating agencies to determine its investment quality. Such a rating would be required by any sophisticated investor.

J.C. Flowers's term sheet, which numbered only a few pages, was relatively informal. The group delivered it to Cohen and Parr, and Chris Flowers fielded a few questions on the details of the bid. But the Bear advisers gave no hint of what they were really thinking; they simply thanked Flowers and walked away.

9:00 P.M.

Paulson was doing a circuit of television talk shows in Washington the following morning, and he wanted to make sure he was up to date on things before he sat for any live interviews. He called Geithner shortly before 9:00 P.M. for an update.

How was Dimon sounding? Paulson wanted to know. Was he comfortable with the thought of buying Bear, despite all the liabilities?

Geithner said he thought so. Dimon had been a little vague, the New York Fed chief said, but there were no signals that he was backing off.

Paulson asked Geithner to notify him immediately if that were to change.

Before he headed home for the night, Schwartz made a personal call to Jamie Dimon. He had heard about the $8 to $12 bid, he told the J.P. Morgan chief, and wanted to know how solid it was. "Are we going to get this done?" Schwartz asked.

Dimon was noncommittal. "I have to talk to my board," he said.

Schwartz found it hard to imagine that Dimon hadn't felt out his directors already—at least on a casual basis. "Jamie," he said, "I don't think any CEO offers anything without talking to their key directors first."

Dimon paused. "I know they want to try to get it done," he said, "but it has to be safe for shareholders. It can't jeopardize the company."

SUNDAY
March 16, 2008

2:00 A.M.

A bleary-eyed Rodge Cohen leafed through the deal papers as he sped home to Irvington early Sunday morning. Lawyers from Wachtell, Lipton, Rosen & Katz, J.P. Morgan's law firm, had e-mailed the term sheets at about 1:30 A.M., and now Cohen was finally getting a close look.

Since the deal price had yet to be finalized, the papers were full of blank lines, but Cohen had expected that. He knew the price range J.P. Morgan was mulling over, and assumed Bear would get the final number later that day—well before the Asian markets started stirring at about 6:00 P.M.

One thing was clear to Cohen: J.P. Morgan wanted assurance. To move forward with such a risky, whirlwind deal, the bank wanted a guarantee that their time and effort wouldn't be wasted. J.P. Morgan didn't want Bear to shop itself around, toying with their price; it wanted a powerful incentive for Bear to stay in the transaction. So as an insurance policy against Bear backing out, J.P. Morgan was asking for a hefty sacrifice if the deal was to fall through: the Madison Avenue building, which was worth at least $1 billion, even in the midst of a distressed market.

As a form of deal protection, it was a pretty aggressive move. Cohen hadn't seen language like that—known in mergers-and-acquisitions parlance as a "crown jewels provision"—in twenty years. Crown jewels clauses, or demands that a company give over its most precious assets in the wake of a broken deal, had been more commonplace in the 1980s. But the Delaware courts, which governed many U.S. corporations, had frowned on the provisions, thinking them unfairly onerous for the target companies, so they had fallen out of vogue.

In more recent years, the standard penalty levied on a company that walked away from a deal was to charge a "breakup fee" high enough to give the target serious pause. But in this case, Bear was so short of cash that J.P. Morgan was substituting its best holdings for money, thinking the firm might not be able to pay a fee by the time the deal was severed.

The proposal wasn't without its advantages. To make sure that Bear's rival firms would continue doing transactions with it, J.P. Morgan was offering to be liable for all of Bear's debts, be they losses from the mortgage portfolio, the cost of being sued over the fallen BSAM hedge funds, or trading losses incurred in the course of day-to-day business.

It was just the sort of assurance that Upton had been hoping for as he looked over the firm's stomach-churning schedule of debts coming due over the next few days. Cohen was surprised by the lengths J.P. Morgan was offering to go to in solidifying market confidence, but pleased that his client would have such protections. It told him J.P. Morgan was in step with reality. To do anything less, he thought, simply wasn't realistic.

Bear, Cohen knew, had a similar objective: certainty of closing. Schwartz and his team couldn't face the thought of this painful weekend of negotiations to be followed by a deal that fell apart. So whatever the price was, and whatever the terms were, they had to be elements that the shareholders could swallow. Cohen prepared himself for what was sure to be another very long day.

7:00 A.M.

Tom Marano had arrived in Manhattan early to take care of some personal business: a meeting at his lawyer's apartment for advice on how to approach the deal negotiations. Bear seemed poised to sell itself to J.P. Morgan, and the mortgage portfolio was at the heart of the price talks. Marano wanted to make sure he bore no personal liability for what had been long held on Bear's balance sheet, and he wanted to protect his own job and wealth without speaking out of turn or selling stock at the wrong time.

Over coffee, Marano's lawyer listened as he explained what had happened over the weekend. The lawyer advised him to take very good notes on every conversation with J.P. Morgan officials. At every meeting, the lawyer explained, Marano should jot down who was there, what was said, and how he or she responded. Marano should keep copies of these notes and share them with the lawyer, so he had a clear record of all the undertakings. He should also get a private telephone and e-mail line so that any future conversations Marano had were not part of Bear or J.P. Morgan's records, as any dealings on his office phone or company e-mail would be.

At 7:14 A.M., an e-mail from Steve Begleiter went out to top Bear managers who were participating in the weekend's talks. Everyone was to meet in the twelfth-floor boardroom promptly at 8:30 A.M., the note said. Alan Schwartz would be there to discuss the state of play.

7:30 A.M.

By the time Vincent Tese had left 383 Madison on Saturday night, things had reached a place of relative calm. Having been posted on the tentative $8 to $12 bid, senior management and directors were hoping for $10 per share, but they knew the final number might well fall at the lower end of that spectrum.

Most of the board had come to accept the bad hand they'd been dealt. But Cayne was going crazy, ranting about how Bear should stick it to the Fed and the Treasury by filing for bankruptcy rather than endure the shame of such a lowball deal.

As the person who was probably closest to Cayne on the board,

Tese was getting an earful. Listening to Cayne yell and sputter over the phone Sunday morning, he decided an intervention was in order. He and Salerno, who was staying at Tese's East Side house to avoid driving back and forth from his own home on Long Island, picked up Cayne at his Park Avenue apartment. Together they drove up to Jackson Hole, a quiet burger joint on Ninety-first and Madison, for a bite to eat.

The directors settled in the brightly lit restaurant, which was decorated with vintage advertisements for Coca-Cola and classic movies. Taxis whizzed up Madison as they talked. Over bacon and eggs, Tese tried to explain to Cayne how hard a bankruptcy filing would be on Bear. Employees would be cut off without a nickel, he argued, and the company's assets would be seized. Not only would shareholders risk being left out to dry, he added, but bondholders would receive nothing. It would be a bad outcome for everyone involved. "Eight dollars is better than zero," he said. "One is better than zero."

Cayne continued to argue, but Tese thought his objections were growing fainter. There was no doubt in his mind that approving whatever deal could be cobbled together that day was very much in Cayne's best interests.

After breakfast, Tese and Salerno dropped Cayne back at his apartment and proceeded to the office, where he would meet them later. Little did they know that the ax was about to fall on the very deal Tese had tried so hard to sell.

Alan Schwartz had already arrived in Midtown and was waiting for a coffee drink in the Starbucks on Forty-eighth Street and Park Avenue, one of the busiest in Manhattan. A long line snaked toward the cash register, and Bob Upton was standing at its tail end, not far from a senior Bear trader. Schwartz hadn't seen his employees walk in.

In fact, standing by the espresso machines in his suit jacket, Schwartz was softly crying. Though he'd been managing the deal talks through the weekend, part of him remained in disbelief.

Schwartz had never thought Bear would perish like this. Keeping himself together in front of employees had been harder than he expected.

The sight put Upton in a dark mood. Whatever negative feelings he'd been able to wall off on Saturday were again bubbling to the surface. He had always felt that in a large company like Bear, the tone was set by those at the top. Schwartz and Molinaro had held up pretty well in public, he felt, and under very rough circumstances. But to know that in a private moment they were in just as much pain as he was—it was almost too much to bear. Instead of making top management seem more human, it had the effect of further depressing Upton.

The treasurer reached the counter and ordered a regular coffee. By the time Schwartz noticed him, Upton was emptying a package of Sweet'n Low into the cup. "Hey, Bob," the CEO said, "I'll walk over with you." They spotted the trader on their way out, who joined them, too.

Schwartz seemed to recover his composure as the three walked the two blocks to Bear's building. J.P. Morgan's team had been incredibly impressed by what they'd seen of Bear's executives, he told Upton and the trader. He sounded optimistic that some sort of deal would get done that weekend.

8:30 A.M.

Schwartz was standing in the twelfth-floor boardroom, surrounded by more than one hundred employees. "We have a deal," he told the group, "but you're not going to like it."

He spoke to the merits of the potential Bear–J.P. Morgan combination. It was the right thing to do, he told the group, and already the cultures seemed to be meshing well, under stressful circumstances. He repeated what he'd said to Upton and the trader: that both the J.P. Morgan executives and the Flowers team had been "impressed with the professionalism of the Bear people" and that praise "meant a lot." Smarting from what they perceived to be a shockingly low bid, some of those listening wondered why the CEO cared.

A few questions were asked, but an air of resignation pervaded. Schwartz said he was aware that some in the stocks and bonds departments had been hesitating to answer all of J.P. Morgan's questions. "I just want to be clear that we can disclose everything," he told the group. It was not the time for holding back, he added, but the time to cooperate as much as possible with an eye toward closing a deal.

Afterward, employees trudged back to their desks and meeting rooms to prepare for another round of grilling. J.P. Morgan was coming in, and Flowers was set to return. But their interest seemed increasingly like a nonissue. As long as J.P. Morgan was interested, it clearly had the upper hand.

Near the Washington Cathedral, Paulson was being picked up by a staff member for the morning shows. He'd asked Geithner to post him if anything had changed on the J.P. Morgan bid for Bear, he told her, and so far, it appeared nothing had. "No news is good news," he said as they sped off.

Although *This Week*, ABC's Sunday morning talk show, wouldn't air until later in the morning, Paulson sat for a pretaped interview at 8:15 A.M. Just minutes in, he was getting hammered over Friday's Fed bailout package.

"Why not set an example of Bear Stearns?" anchor George Stephanopoulos asked. "The guys who have this record of dog-eat-dog, we're brass knuckles, we're tough. This is the perfect time to set an example. . . . You say you're aware of moral hazard, but it does seem like you're creating one."

"Well, every situation is different," began Paulson. "We have to respond to the circumstances we're facing today. And my concern is to minimize the impact on the broader economy as we work our way through this situation, and again, the stability of our financial system. That's—"

Stephanopoulos interrupted. "What would happen if Bear Stearns didn't get this loan?"

"I'm not going to speculate, George," Paulson replied. He defended the Fed's decision. What the pundits would say the following day if more bailout money were extended, he could only imagine.

"I think the big question on a lot of people's minds is, are there other banks in a situation similar to Bear Stearns's right now?" Stephanopoulos asked. "Is this just the beginning?"

"Well, our financial institutions, our banks and investment banks, are very strong," Paulson said. "And I'm convinced that they're going to come out of this situation very strong. Our markets are resilient. They're flexible. I'm quite confident we're going to work our way through this situation."

Apparently having exhausted his Bear questions, Stephanopoulos moved on to the housing crisis.

It was a grueling television circuit. Paulson's other two interviewers, Fox News anchor Chris Wallace and CNN's Wolf Blitzer, grilled him about both the Fed loan and the state of the banking business in general. An overwhelming number of economists polled by the *Wall Street Journal* thought the economy was in a recession, they pointed out, and with Bear's teetering status, the entire Wall Street business model seemed potentially at risk. Who was next? both wanted to know.

At one point, Blitzer became confrontational. "Tell the taxpayers who are watching right now why you decided to bail out, in effect, Bear Stearns, the fifth-largest investment house in the United States, which, only a couple of days ago, seemed to be on the verge of collapse, primarily because of its investments in . . . mortgages, which are obviously a disaster," he said.

"Well, to—again, to step back," replied Paulson, "I have great,

great confidence in our capital markets and in our financial institutions." After reiterating that, he added that "we've been going through turmoil in the capital markets for a while."

"Why did you bail out Bear Stearns?" Blitzer demanded.

Paulson stammered. "There are ongoing discussions right now," he said. "I've been on the phone for a couple of days straight, throughout the weekend." He stopped, not wanting to say too much. He reminded himself to stay on message. He was preoccupied with what would happen to Bear that day, but couldn't divulge that on national television.

"I'm not going to project right now what the outcome of that situation is," he finally said.

After more circular discussion, Blitzer hit on the money question. "If you wouldn't have bailed out Bear Stearns, what would have happened?" he asked.

"Wolf, I'm not going to speculate about what-ifs," Paulson said. "Our number-one priority," he added, "is to minimize instability, minimize spillover into the real economy."

"Secretary Paulson," Blitzer said, "you have got a huge problem on your shoulders right now. Good luck."

9:00 A.M.

Over at 270 Park, it had not been a good night.

Dimon and other top executives had spent the evening moving to and from the office suites on the executive floor, comparing thoughts on the due diligence their teams were performing. The initial reports on Bear's health had been good, but as the night wore on and the answers to second and third rounds of detail questions came back, the group became uneasy.

For one thing, there was the mortgage portfolio, which seemed to be full of shaky assets. J.P. Morgan had asked Marano and his people a number of follow-up questions on what they held, and the answers had not been forthcoming. Here was Bear's biggest liability, the bank officials thought, and we're not getting straight answers.

By Sunday morning, the senior team was operating on little or no sleep, and their offices were a mess. Some had caught a little rest on the eighth floor's uncomfortable upholstered couches, but not enough to feel refreshed. Dinner had been ordered in, and the conference rooms were now strewn with pizza boxes and empty red wine bottles. A certain degree of confusion reined. Because of the executive floor's sprawling design, individuals could be hard to find, forcing people to wander from room to room until they found whomever they were looking for.

As they pored over the information from Bear, Black had grown increasingly skeptical. He and his cochief of the investment bank, Bill Winters, would be largely responsible for any Bear operations the bank acquired. And while the deal seemed appealingly cheap, the target company had a lot of problems. Black was feeling increasingly ambivalent.

The morning's *New York Times*, however, crystallized his thinking. In a column written by Gretchen Morgenson, the investigative journalist who had broken much of the news about the A.R. Baron and Stratton Oakmont scandals, the *Times* argued that a government bailout ran greatly afoul of the public interest. Dubbing the Federal Reserve "Rescues 'R' Us," the paper reminded readers about Bear's scandalous past and its devil-may-care attitude toward doing business with its brethren on the Street, noting the firm's refusal to participate in the Long-Term Capital industry bailout as well as its failure to oversee the two failed hedge funds.

Then, the clincher: Bear had a recorded $46 billion of mortgage assets on its balance sheet, which in a bankruptcy scenario would be dumped into a frozen market, potentially creating havoc for other investors and banks, the *Times* pointed out. But it was unclear, the paper added, what that portfolio really contained. At least $17 billion of the holdings had been valued using the best judgment of Marano and his team, rather than by benchmarking the assets against other market prices.* That left a big question mark over what the securities might really be worth. Perhaps the $17 billion of assets that hadn't been independently valued were, in fact, close to zero under distressed conditions. That still left roughly $30 billion in other assets that had been valued using accepted market prices, but were no doubt still declining as conditions in the housing sector worsened.

The article all but confirmed Black's biggest concerns—and let him know that the public was watching closely, in case he had any doubts.

Shortly after 9:00, Black addressed Dimon, Cutler, and other executives. "Look, I'm very concerned," he told the group, "and other people have reflected the same view." He cited the *Times* story that morning and the concerns he was having about the very same points.†

Dimon's mind was made up: "We're not going to be able to do a deal under these terms," he said.

Jamie Dimon, now fifty-two, had never been afraid of saying no. A rebellious Harvard Business School graduate from Queens, he had come of age professionally under the tutelage of Sanford I. Weill, the brash former broker who created the financial supermarket Citigroup Inc. In graduate school, Dimon scored points with classmates for demonstrating a professor's analytical error on the blackboard

---

*This type of valuation, which had become common in certain parts of the fixed-income market, was sometimes the only option for "less liquid," or less frequently traded, assets. Because the assets didn't change hands very often, there were often no easily observable prices at a given time, leaving it to experienced traders to make their best guesses.

†Tom Marano, Bear's head of mortgage, has told associates that the first he heard of J.P. Morgan's doubts about his valuations was not that weekend but during the middle of the following week. Until then, it appeared to him that diligence was proceeding smoothly.

just two weeks into the first semester. His future wife, a fellow B-school student named Judy, was attracted to his cool remove. The night they met at a Boston area bar, "the room was a sea of Ivy Leaguers in pastel Lacoste shirts, all grinning, all trying to win each other over," she later recalled. "He was sphinxlike, taking things in, not trying to be a part of the group."

Dimon was exposed to the financial world at a young age. His father, Theodore "Ted" Dimon, worked as a broker at Shearson Hammill & Co., an old-line retail firm where his own father, Panos, a Greek immigrant, also worked. When Shearson was acquired by Weill's firm, Hayden Stone, in the early 1970s, Ted Dimon developed a quick rapport with the new boss.

As a teenager, Jamie spent time at his father's office during the summer, overhearing the shoptalk that went on around him. In college, he wrote a paper about Weill's acquisition of Shearson; when Weill, who had seen a copy of the paper, praised his work, Dimon hit him up for a job. He was hired that summer as a junior worker in the budget department. Some years later, he turned down job offers from Goldman, Morgan Stanley, and Lehman Brothers in favor of a role at American Express—the company that had bought Shearson—as Weill's personal assistant.

Dimon quickly became Weill's right arm. In 1986, after Weill had been ousted from American Express on the heels of a power dispute, he and Dimon engineered new roles for themselves at the struggling consumer loan company Commercial Credit. A backwater operation based in Baltimore, Commercial Credit nonetheless had a wide network of clients and revenues of more than $1 billion per year. The two saw potential.

Not long after turning Commercial Credit around, Weill and Dimon began laying the groundwork for a triumphant return to New York. In 1988, Commercial Credit bought Primerica, the former can manufacturer that then owned the respected retail brokerage Smith Barney, among other holdings. Soon after, Weill also bought pieces of Drexel Burnham Lambert, the hard-driving brokerage and investment bank that was by then mired in scandal and soon to fail.

In the 1990s, Dimon's rise to the top echelons of Wall Street continued as he followed his boss back to New York. Weill had repurchased Shearson from American Express and taken over the troubled insurer Travelers, whose name he kept for his parent company. In 1997, Weill also bought Salomon Inc., the parent company of the fabled bond-trading powerhouse Salomon Brothers. His crowning achievement, however, occurred in 1998 with the $83 billion merger of Travelers and Citicorp, the enormous bank and credit-card concern. The deal combined assets of $700 billion and employee ranks that would swell to more than 161,000. Moreover, the merged entities combined so many disparate aspects of financial services—insurance, commercial banking, and stock trading, among many others—that it required a rethinking of federal regulations that had kept such functions separate since the Great Depression.

Dimon, whose talents as an executive and a number cruncher were by then well known, was excited about the transformative deal, which created the umbrella company Citigroup Inc. But just a month after it was finalized, he got some unpleasant news: Weill and John Reed, the acerbic Citicorp CEO who was now jointly heading the combined company, wanted Dimon out.

Despite his chagrin, Dimon went gracefully, encouraging Citi employees to keep working hard. He even shouldered some of the blame for his personality clashes in a press conference that day. But Dimon's exit did not sit well with some of the company's other managers. Steve Black, then a vice chairman at Salomon Smith Barney, Citi's brokerage arm, resigned in protest after voicing his anger to Weill. Salomon's trading floor offered Dimon a standing ovation on the day he arrived to pack up his things. Afterward, about one hundred senior employees toasted his work at a restaurant nearby.

Dimon had by then made it big. He lived in a posh Park Avenue apartment with Judy and their three daughters, who attended an exclusive Manhattan girls' school. On his departure, Citigroup gave him $30 million in severance. And he now had a chance to restart his career, if he chose to.

The next few years were a throwback to the time that had elapsed between Dimon's and Weill's time together at American Express and Commercial Credit: a long, slow search for the right opportunity. Dimon rented space in the Seagram Building, the fancy East Side skyscraper that housed the Four Seasons restaurant, and the same place he and his mentor had worked after their departure from American Express. He began taking boxing lessons. He made a list of things he'd like to do if he had his druthers: become a full-time investor, a teacher, an author, even a stay-at-home dad. In the end, though, he could not abandon his penchant for financial services.

In 2000, Dimon was recruited by Chicago's Bank One, the Midwest's largest bank, to become CEO. The country's third-biggest credit-card issuer, Bank One was nonetheless a sleepy, poorly managed behemoth that was struggling to find a strategy when Dimon came on board. He relocated his family to Chicago, where they moved into a twenty-six-room mansion, and set to work. "This was my one big shot," he later told *Fortune*. "How many times will big banks change their CEOs in the next three or four years, and of these, how many will hire an outsider?"

Bank One was a mess. Risky loans had helped juice revenues, and when the company noticed one or two late credit-card payments, it was known to bump its interest charges up to rapacious rates, seemingly overnight. Profits had not been stable. In 2000, the year Dimon was hired, Bank One reported a loss of $511 million.

Dimon began paring expenses and assessing the bank's product models, making its business lines more efficient. He took pains to improve management's work ethic, setting his own example by working ambitious hours and calling senior people when he was on the road to make sure they hadn't cut out early. He improved the company's computer technology, believing better systems would help the company make strategic deals. Visiting Bank One's branches around the country, he questioned employees on how they felt about their superiors, always looking for ways to improve. "What do I think of our competitors?" he asked a group of middle managers at a bank gathering in 2002. "I hate them! I want them to bleed!" By 2003, Bank One reported $3.5 billion in profits.

Early in 2004, Dimon got the ultimate break: to be the future CEO of J.P. Morgan. In a $58 billion deal, Morgan and Bank One had agreed to merge, and the New York commercial bank's CEO, William Harrison, was soon to retire. If Dimon could sit tight for two years, he was told, he could succeed Harrison in 2006. Dimon was forty-seven.

With combined assets of $1.1 trillion, the two banks would give Citi, which then had $1.2 trillion, a run for its money. But J.P. Morgan, like Bank One when Dimon arrived, was facing some hard times. Four years after the 2000 merger of J.P. Morgan, the blue chip commercial and investment bank, and Chase Manhattan Corporation, the large commercial bank, the resultant company had struggled with venture-capital losses, bad loans, and embarrassing relationships with the scorned companies Enron and WorldCom.

Dimon was named president and chief operating officer when the deal closed that summer of 2004. That fall, the patchy bond market helped push J.P. Morgan's earnings down significantly from the year before, a performance Dimon described to investors as "terrible." Doubts surfaced about whether having a future CEO like Dimon waiting in the wings could lead to a power struggle.

Now in the all-too-familiar role of number two at a large corporation, Dimon yet again embarked on a major round of cuts—or "waste-cutting," as he described it. Cell phones and pagers became an employee expense, with only the business calls reimbursable. Workers who had been on thirty-five-hour-per-week schedules were switched to forty-hour weeks. Health-care premiums rose for better-compensated workers, and some of the bank's charitable donations were pared back as well.

In the months that followed, J.P. Morgan settled with plaintiffs in the major Enron and WorldCom cases, hoping to put the matters behind it. By the end of the year, profits were growing, but a continued, spotty performance in the trading unit dragged down overall results. On January 1, 2006, six months before the originally planned date, Dimon was named J.P. Morgan's CEO. For his work the previous year, his take-home pay had been $22 million.

Over the next two years, Dimon positioned J.P. Morgan to weather the credit crisis better than most of his peers on Wall Street were doing at their respective firms. Thinking the returns too low, he and his investment-bank chiefs, which now included Bill Winters and his old friend Steve Black, steered the bank away from risky holdings like structured investment vehicles and CDOs. At a time when the subprime-mortgage market was on fire, J.P. Morgan made few loans to borrowers with poor credit, protecting its balance sheet from future losses. (The bank did make a big push, however, into credit cards that catered to such consumers.) Instead, J.P. Morgan sought to broaden its reach in retail banking around the country, hoping to compete with larger rivals, like Bank of America. Dimon's goals were simple and straightforward: Grow profits, and avoid stepping in shit. "Forget the visionary stuff," he told the *Wall Street Journal* shortly after his promotion. J.P. Morgan, he added, "should be growing salespeople, traders, bankers, marketing, innovation, and new-product extensions."

By early 2007, J.P. Morgan's performance was far stronger. Profits for the prior year were $14.4 billion, an all-time record, and Dimon took home a pay package of $27 million. Buoyed by what were also record results in the investment bank, net income rose dramatically during the first quarter of the year, increasing confidence in the bank. In the third quarter, J.P. Morgan's profits ticked up slightly, while results at Citi—by then its biggest competitor—sank by 57 percent. By early 2008, the firm had again churned out record profits for the previous year, this time topping $15 billion.

Unlike at Citi, at J.P. Morgan Dimon's personal style seemed to energize the culture, a mix of old-school investment bankers from "heritage" J.P. Morgan and less affected commercial bankers from Chase Manhattan. Internal meetings with Dimon were short and to the point, and he never hesitated to embarrass a colleague who had made a bad call. "That's the dumbest thing I ever heard," he was known to say, even to senior executives. On one occasion, he told a bunch of J.P. Morgan internal auditors that a female associate of his "knows about as much accounting in her baby finger as all of you combined." To Dimon, conceit was a cancer that could ruin institutions. A large company like J.P. Morgan risked getting "arrogant and full of hubris and lose focus, like the Roman Empire," he told *Fortune* in a 2006 interview. The solution, he felt, was tying compensation to merit and insisting on regular, rigorous scrutiny of individual managers and the businesses they handled. This was necessary because "in a big company, it's easy for people to b.s. you. A lot of them have been practicing for decades." (It was a phenomenon Dimon was on high alert for when he arrived at Bank One. "The worst [managers] showed up at my door the first day to bullshit me," he told *Fortune* at that time.)

Dimon's one-liners weren't restricted to the office. "He loves misbehaving in places where he's supposed to behave," Judy Dimon once told a reporter. One infamous confrontation occurred at a Citi black-tie event in 1998, not long before Dimon was forced out of the company. As a gesture of goodwill, Steve Black had begun dancing with the wife of Deryck Maughan, another senior executive at Citi, with whom Black did not get along. Instead of reciprocating the gesture, however, Maughan abandoned Black's wife, Debbie, on the dance floor. An enraged Black was yelling at Maughan about the incident when Dimon stepped in. Grabbing Maughan, Dimon said, "Either you intended to snub Blackie's wife or you didn't. Which is it?"

Maughan tried to break away, but Dimon spun him around, popping a button off his shirt. "Don't you ever turn your back on me when I'm talking!" he yelled, prompting Maughan's wife to scream, "This man is attacking my husband!" Dimon later apologized to Maughan, but the damage was done.*

On Sunday morning Geithner was in his office on the thirteenth floor of the New York Fed building when Dimon called to tell him they were backing off. "There's just no way," the J.P. Morgan chief said. "There's just a much bigger hole than we thought."

Bear had far riskier assets than the bank had initially realized, Dimon explained, and he just couldn't rationalize taking on that sort of risk after a mere weekend of due diligence. The mortgage portfolio, with its hard-to-value assets, was of special concern. "The math doesn't work for us," Dimon said. "I can't do something that's going to imperil my firm."

Geithner tried to argue with Dimon, but the J.P. Morgan chief was unmoving. Privately, Geithner was surprised. He had spent an enormous amount of time on the phone with Dimon that weekend, walking him through the various deal scenarios and risks, and he had not expected the bank chief to blink.

Hanging up with Dimon, Geithner phoned Bernanke and Paulson in Washington. He relayed to the officials what the J.P. Morgan chief had just told him. "We've heard from Jamie, and he can't do it," Geithner told the officials.

Paulson's reaction was immediate. "We can't let it go," he said.

Geithner concurred. He also thought there might be a way to help. "But there is one thing I need to tell you about," he added.

---

*A memorable confrontation over Bear's travails would occur on Sunday, March 16, in a call Dimon held with industry executives. On being asked a skeptical question by Citi chief executive Vikram Pandit, Dimon responded gruffly that Pandit should "stop being such a jerk."

"They have thirty billion dollars in assets they don't want to take."
He described the mortgage portfolio and what was in it.

The officials talked the situation through. If J.P. Morgan was
turned off by the mortgage portfolio, Geithner wondered, could the
Fed somehow step in to reassure them? On Friday, the central bank
had invoked a rarely used section of the Federal Reserve Act in order
to accept potentially risky assets from Bear as collateral for the loan
it planned to issue through J.P. Morgan. That clause, applicable only
in "unusual or exigent circumstances," meant the Fed could autho-
rize lending to reserve banks if a firm was unable to secure loans
from other banking institutions—making the central bank the
lender of last resort. Under the same thinking, Geithner suggested,
perhaps the Fed could somehow guarantee the $30 billion portfolio
in order to help a sale go through.

Bernanke was incredulous. Two days ago, he had stretched his
powers further than any Fed chairman had in decades, and already
he was being asked to do the same thing again. It was the exact issue
Stephanopoulos had railed about to Paulson the day before. But increasingly, it felt that his hands were tied. The doomsday scenarios
that had been discussed on Friday still applied. Bear's one realistic
buyer was now backing away. If these weren't exigent circumstances,
what were?

9:30 A.M.

Steve Black was on the phone with Schwartz, telling him they were
on hold until more satisfactory terms could be reached.

"You've known me a long time," the J.P. Morgan executive told
the Bear chief. "This is not posturing."

To Schwartz, sitting in his forty-second-floor office, Black
sounded dead serious. Schwartz had an enormous problem on his
hands. The J.C. Flowers investment consortium had gotten basically

nowhere, and Morgan and Goldman hadn't even begun to perform their due diligence on Bear's prime brokerage. Meanwhile, the clock was ticking. The opening of the Asian markets, which signaled the end of the line for Bear, was only nine hours away.

After a night's consideration, Black explained, J.P. Morgan was nowhere close to $8 to $12 per share. Anything the bank might do, he said, would be under radically different terms. His advice to Schwartz was to pursue any and all other options Bear might have. "You can't count on us," Black said.

Schwartz was genteel on the phone, but once again, he was shaken. He called Cohen and Parr into his office.

Rocking back in his chair, he relayed the conversation. "We've got a real problem," Schwartz said. "I just heard from Steve Black. They've run the models. They think the hole is huge, and they're not sure they can do a deal without government support."

Parr was hesitant. "Do you think they were just negotiating?" he asked.

"Perhaps," Schwartz said. "But I think they're very serious. I don't know how they could have possibly gotten there, but I believe they're serious."

Cohen asked if Schwartz had talked to the government about J.P. Morgan's sudden reticence.

"No," said Schwartz. "I wanted to talk to the two of you first."

"I'm sure they've been posted by J.P. Morgan on this," Cohen said. "I don't expect the government to back them out of their position." In other words, the Fed wasn't going to talk J.P. Morgan into a deal.

Cohen went into another room and began calling some of his government contacts. He explained his client's consternation over the apparently broken deal.

"We can't tell Chase what to do," one of the Fed contacts argued.

"We've got to have a transaction," Cohen replied.

His contact was clear: Bear should do what it had to do—explore a deal with someone else, consider dropping the price—but the Fed wasn't going to twist J.P. Morgan's arm on Bear's behalf.

For the second time in seventy-two hours, Bear was on the edge of bankruptcy. Chapter 11 papers would again have to be compiled.

Dennis Block, the Cadwalader lawyer, hadn't worked such round-the-clock hours on a deal in years. He'd left the building at 2:00 A.M. the previous night, around the same time as Cohen, and had driven home to Long Island, where he barely had time to shower, shave, and catch a catnap before turning around again. Now he dispatched his bankruptcy team downtown to his firm's offices at the World Financial Center. He feared that the specter of lawyers working on a Chapter 11 filing would cast a pall over the deal negotiations at Bear, where some hope still existed.

Noon

Three days after David Solomon, Goldman's co-head of investment banking, had called Molinaro to offer assistance, a team from the downtown firm had finally been invited by Flowers to 383. But late that morning, word filtered to Jacob Goldfield, one of the private-equity shop's senior team members, that the Goldman team was having trouble getting in.

A former star trader at Goldman who knew many of its senior players, Goldfield shot an e-mail to Goldman CEO Lloyd Blankfein, who was at home on the Upper East Side. There was no problem with the Goldman group coming over, Goldfield wrote. Blankfein should tell them to come on ahead.

Blankfein replied with his phone number.

Goldfield called the CEO to find him enraged. Blankfein's team couldn't "get into the building," he said, and had been waiting "for hours." The whole situation was an insult, Blankfein felt, and needed to be addressed right away. Goldfield assured him that the team was welcome.

Shortly after that, the Goldman team was let in, and Goldfield and John Oros, another Goldman alum working with the Flowers team that weekend, were summoned to meet with the them in a conference room on the twelfth floor. Gathered around the table were firm president Gary Cohn, head of credit Don Mullen, and a handful of others. After a few minutes of chatter, Cohn jumped in.

"I suppose you expect us to sign a confidentiality agreement," he said.

Goldfield and Oros were taken aback. Signing a confidentiality, or nondisclosure, agreement, was simply part of the deal process. It ensured that if a company revealed nonpublic information about its revenue, expenses, or cash position, the data would stay under wraps afterward. Flowers had signed a confidentiality accord with Bear, and it was presumed that if Goldman came to 383 at Flowers's behest, Goldman would do so, too.

If Goldman was going to enter into a confidential process, the Flowers team told Cohn, he would have to sign.

"Well, we're not going to sign it," Cohn replied. Goldman didn't want to be bound to any rules about not poaching Bear executives who might be in play as a result of the company's sale, he said—partly because Goldman was already holding talks with the people it wanted.

Goldfield and Oros conveyed that they had signed a confidentiality agreement, and that if Goldman didn't follow suit, the Flowers group would not be able to let the firm in on what its plans for Bear might be. Cohn was not dissuaded.

After a few more minutes of arguing, Goldfield and Oros gave up, telling Cohn they would report his feelings to their colleagues and see what could be done next. Since they couldn't get past square one with Goldman, there seemed little point to the Flowers team in continuing the conversation.[*]

By the time his team members were upstairs arguing with Cohn about the nondisclosure agreement, it had already become apparent to Chris Flowers that he was probably out of the running. He was wasting a weekend at the Bear offices, he rationalized, just in case J.P. Morgan changed its mind. If it did, Flowers could buy Bear for a pittance, keep the organization and its management largely intact, and, when things turned around, make an absolute fortune. But that scenario seemed increasingly unlikely.

Throughout the day, Flowers and his group hung around Cayne's office and his windowless conference room, looking casually at the information they'd already gathered about Bear's assets and liabilities. Parr checked in on the group every hour or two to see if they had any questions. It seemed to Flowers like a pointless exercise, even though he appreciated the gesture.

Despite the fire drills going on in other parts of the building, the Flowers team was unruffled. They had worked out their blueprint for a deal, submitted it the prior evening, and all they could do now was wait.

Sometime after the Goldman group's argument with Goldfield and Oros, Molinaro walked down to Cayne's office suite, where the Flowers team was camped out. Goldman, it seemed, had remained in the building and was now asking for information on Bear's mortgage portfolio, and Molinaro was looking for guidance on what, exactly, to show them. After all, he thought Goldman was in the building at the Flowers group's behest, so they should be calling the shots, it seemed.

---

[*]Cohn says through a spokesman that he and his colleagues had no trouble getting into the Bear building that day and that he can't recall being asked to sign a confidentiality agreement.

"We'd like to be helpful [to the Goldman group,]" Molinaro explained. "How would you like us to help?"

It had been strange for Molinaro to see the Goldman guys walk in, asking questions and chewing gum. Don Mullen had once been a senior player in Bear's fixed-income division before switching firms in 2001. Now, just like Solomon had, he was calling on his old firm to offer a life preserver, a humiliating situation for his former colleague.

The Flowers group was confused by Molinaro's question. They had asked Goldman over to get some general advice and to show them the prime-brokerage assets. Looking puzzled, a Flowers employee finally told Molinaro that they weren't aware of Goldman's interest in the entire firm and weren't sure how to advise him. It seemed best to just have Goldman deal directly with Bear.

Cohn, who had remained upstairs, couldn't believe how chaotic the situation was. It seemed to him that Goldman had been getting mixed messages all weekend. Yes, they'd been asked about their interest in the prime brokerage. But the firm had also been under the impression that all of Bear was for sale, and that Goldman should consider a purchase. Knowing the importance of Bear's mortgage portfolio, Cohn had amassed a team of fixed-income traders to help do a quick valuation of those assets. They were standing by at his firm's New York Plaza tower, waiting for the data to be sent over. But now Goldman was having a hard time getting access to the numbers they wanted.

1:00 P.M.

Marano spent most of Sunday sitting through more presentations. By that point, his mind had strayed from Bear to what would happen next: a scramble for his team to find new positions at J.P. Morgan, a grueling integration process, and, more likely than not, litigation over the deal.

During his lunch break he walked down to the AT&T store on the ground level of the building and bought himself an iPhone for personal use. He encouraged friends to do the same.

For the board, that afternoon was a whirlwind. Grasping at any possible reprieve, directors and management worked the phones, touching base with all their government and Wall Street contacts to ask for advice and help. Schwartz kept in touch with Bob Steel, now back in Washington, and Kevin Warsh. Cohen kept in touch with Geithner. Both were desperate for Bear to get a decent deal.

J.P. Morgan, however, was still on the fence. Having abandoned the original deal price, Dimon and his team were now considering some far lower numbers, if they were to go ahead at all.

Geithner was in near-constant touch with Dimon, who had shared his thinking with the New York Fed president. In the middle of the afternoon, he called Paulson to give the Treasury secretary an update. Given the promise of Fed assistance in protecting the company from losses on the mortgage portfolio, a J.P. Morgan deal again looked promising, he said. But the deal price would be considerably lower than what had been discussed on Saturday night. "Shareholders are going to get between $3 and $5 a share," Geithner said. Over at J.P. Morgan, in fact, the figure $4 was strongly in play.

"How could that be?" Paulson asked. For a company in such distress, that seemed far too high to him.* He hadn't needed the morning's talk shows to remind him of the risk of moral hazard: giving taxpayers the impression that poorly managed companies would be bailed out by the government, at their expense.

Geithner said he had tried to make that point to Dimon. Still, he thought Paulson should call the J.P. Morgan chief directly.

Dimon answered Paulson's call from a speakerphone box. He got right to the point: Bear had been on the verge of bankruptcy when

---

*Days later, Paulson told Dimon in a conversation about the deal that "[the idea of J.P. Morgan paying $10 per share for Bear] makes me want to vomit."

the government and J.P. Morgan had stepped in, he said. To actually reward Bear's investors for allowing their company to be run into the ground seemed unfathomable.

"I can't see why they're getting anything," Paulson argued. "I could see something nominal, like one or two dollars per share."

2:00 P.M.

Tom Wipf, a senior manager in Morgan Stanley's financing department, was doing some work on his home computer in the Park Slope section of Brooklyn when he got a call from his boss. Bear had invited Morgan to come in and value its prime-brokerage business for a possible quick acquisition, the higher-up said. Wipf should gather a few colleagues and be at 383 within the hour.

He hopped on the subway and was there by 3:00 with about a half dozen other Morgan treasury and financing managers in tow. They were escorted up to the sixth floor, where Molinaro and a team from Bear's prime-brokerage unit had assembled to field questions on their hedge fund client-services business. Goldman's Cohn, the Morgan team learned, was in another room as they spoke, conducting a similar session. The managers had been part of competitive deal negotiations before, but this felt surreal.

The Bear group was frank about what they were up against. Key clients had been pulling cash throughout the week, they acknowledged, and they expected the exodus to continue unless investors could somehow be reassured. They showed Wipf and his colleagues the list. The damage was bad, indeed.

Worsening matters was the fact that many of Bear's trading rivals had stopped lending stock to it—rendering Bear unable to provide clients with shares they wanted to borrow in order to sell stocks "short," or bet that they would fall.

The Morgan team was sympathetic to the Bear managers. They

were in an unenviable situation. Clients had flown away the prior week, and no doubt Bear would be facing more notifications of departures on Monday. Doing a deal didn't seem to make much sense if the key players were bailing out, Wipf thought, but he respected Bear for exploring all its options.

After about two hours, the meeting ended uneventfully. Bear had other suitors to deal with, and Morgan felt there wasn't much left to buy anyway.

Upstairs in a conference room on the forty-third floor, one floor above Schwartz's office, the board members were gathered. Carl Glickman, still recovering from a stroke and confined to a wheelchair, had flown in from Cleveland, accompanied by his male nurse and his wife, Babs, and Salerno had returned from Florida. Greenberg, Nickell, Tese, and Michael Goldstein, the former chairman of Toys 'R' Us, were also there. Those who couldn't make it in person were being dialed in for periodic conference calls.

Cohen was still in touch with his government contacts, who, hours after J.P. Morgan had abruptly walked away from the talks, said there might be renewed interest in a deal. Dimon had expressed a willingness to reconsider, Cohen was told, if the government was willing to backstop the mortgage assets. Some sort of Fed guarantee of Bear's mortgage portfolio, the contacts told Cohen, was probably in the works.

Bear's advisers wanted directors to be prepared for an eleventh-hour bid that would leave little time for deliberation. So together, Cohen and Peter Atkins, the veteran deals lawyer from Skadden, Arps, Slate, Meagher & Flom who had advised the RJR Nabisco board on its leveraged buyout in the late 1980s, briefed the board on their duties as directors. Atkins had been called in by Schwartz, who knew and liked him from working on past deals, and he, too, was assisting the Bear board in its decision making.

Traditionally, the board's obligation would be to act in the best interests of a company's shareholders. But Bear's deteriorating position made matters more complicated. The firm wasn't yet out of money, but it was getting close. Based on the balance sheet, or the cash it had on paper, Bear looked as though it could continue to operate for some time to come. But in the other test of solvency—whether Bear could pay its debts as they came due—the firm failed. With as much as $50 billion of short-term loans to be replenished on Monday, Bear's situation was exceedingly tenuous. That meant that in making a decision on any J.P. Morgan bid, directors would have to consider the interests of bondholders, who held Bear's corporate debt, as well as shareholders.

Dire as he knew the situation was, however, Marano wasn't convinced that Bear's executives had examined all their options. What about a management buyout, in which the top brass took over their own company? Had the firm totally ruled out a bankruptcy filing, which it knew the government wanted to avoid? Had Bear reached out to some of its institutional contacts in Europe, to see if there might be a good transcontinental fit?

With these ideas in mind, Marano, Mayer, and several other fixed-income traders went down to the sixth floor to talk to Schwartz and Metrick.

In the room, the traders began laying out their ideas, including management buyout and the prospects for Chapter 11. But just minutes into their discussion, Schwartz began screaming at the traders.

"What do you think we are, idiots?" he asked. "Of course we've thought of that!" Unbeknownst to the traders, Schwartz had long since abandoned the alternatives, and was now staring down a J.P. Morgan deal at a paltry sum.

The traders tried to hold their ground. They had heard word of J.P. Morgan's rapidly declining bid price, and thought Bear could do better than just a few dollars per share. "If we filed for bankruptcy, you would get more," Marano said.

Schwartz was having none of it. After fifteen minutes, he abruptly ended the meeting, leaving the traders to wait it out.

Marano was outraged at the way he and his colleagues had been treated. As he walked out of the room, he pulled Metrick aside.

He expected better from Schwartz, he told the investment banker. "I would advise you to tell him not to raise his voice to anybody ever again," Marano warned, "because during the events of the last twenty-four hours, he has lost his right to raise his voice to anybody."

4:00 P.M.

Cayne, who had arrived at the building around lunchtime, continued to object heatedly. "Let's play the bankruptcy card," he said repeatedly to the other board members. Hoping to talk some sense into him, Block, whose opinion Cayne had always respected, pulled him aside and told him in no uncertain terms that bankruptcy was not an option.

Cayne felt strongly that the intrinsic value of Bear was far greater than ten or fewer dollars per share. But something about Block's pleas seemed to change his mind. Fond as he was of Tese, Cayne needed to hear the argument against bankruptcy from other parties. He seemed to respect the lawyers, who had decades of experience in securities deals.

Cayne and Block, who, at sixty-five, was ten years younger, went way back. In 1987, Bear had sued the Hong Kong investment bank Jardine Strategic Holdings Limited after the firm abandoned a plan to take a 20 percent investment in Bear. The deal had been inked, but not finalized, before the market crash that October, and after Bear's shares hurtled downward alongside many blue chip stocks, Jardine had argued that it was no longer worth the price to which the companies had agreed.

Bear's lawyer at the time, the distinguished Arthur Liman, felt it didn't stand a chance. But Cayne, then an up-and-coming player in Bear's senior management ranks, wanted to fight. Block thought Bear could win its case, so Cayne hired Block to take on Jardine. Four years later, just weeks before the trial was set to begin, Jardine settled the matter out of court for $60 million.

Inside the conference room, directors were making small talk between presentations. It was a nail-biting period. The opening of the Asian markets was just a few hours away, and no deal was yet in sight.

Parr walked the board through his steps over the weekend, listing the suitors he had called and what their responses had been. It boiled down to few options other than J.P. Morgan or bankruptcy. Bear had welcomed the Flowers overture, but the government had signaled strongly that without a consortium of banks to back up the private-equity bid, the bid was no good.

Around 4:00, Parr stepped out to take a call from J.P. Morgan. It was Doug Braunstein, their chief deal maker, calling him with an updated bid. Bear and J.P. Morgan were back in the game, but at a far lower price.

Parr returned to the conference room. "There's a three-party deal," he told the directors. "There's a deal between us and J.P. Morgan. They're getting certain backstops from the Fed.

"The deal is not at eight or twelve dollars," he continued. "It's four dollars."

The directors exchanged surprised looks. How had J.P. Morgan gotten to $4? several board members asked.

J.P. Morgan had felt there was too much risk in the deal to pay more, Parr said. Some directors doubted that. They had thought Bear was a steal at $8, and now the bid was half of that. This is political, thought Tese. He suspected that Paulson had directed the price downward. Others felt the same way.

Less than an hour later, Parr's cell phone rang again. He stepped out.

It was Braunstein again. "The number's two dollars," the banker said.

Parr could hardly believe it. "Surely you don't mean that," he replied. Braunstein held firm.

Parr returned to the room and relayed the new price. Directors were astonished. Cayne, still not quite convinced, repeated his objections.

Cohen was astounded. He stepped out into a hallway and called a Fed official on his cell phone.

"It's outrageous," he told the official, referring to the revised price. "We would have no choice," he said, "but to disclose in a filing that the Fed forced a sale at two dollars." Bear would have to file with the SEC a proxy statement, or informational document, explaining the deal it had done with J.P. Morgan to investors. And Cohen would ensure that it said the government had mandated a low price.

Tese addressed the group. "I want to vomit over the price," he said, "but we have zero alternatives." Privately, he had his doubts about whether the shareholders would accept $2 in a vote. But that was something they'd deal with down the road.

"Two dollars is better than nothing," Schwartz agreed. The board, he felt, had little choice. The Fed and the Treasury clearly wanted Bear to be sold to J.P. Morgan to ward off a market-wide meltdown. Visions of bankruptcy filled his head: padlocked offices, paychecks that would immediately cease to arrive. There was more at play here than just the shareholders' interests, he knew.

For half an hour, Schwartz made his case to the board. Bear needed to go for a solid deal, he argued, rather than risk the consequences of bankruptcy. When he was finished, he took the vote.

"All in favor?" Schwartz asked.

The group voiced their consent.

"Do I have anyone who's opposed?" he asked.

There was silence.

7:00 P.M.

At 7:05, the deal was announced to the world.

"J.P. Morgan Chase & Co. announced it is acquiring The Bear Stearns Companies Inc.," read a press release issued by both firms. "Directors of both companies have unanimously approved the transaction."

As part of the deal, the release noted, J.P. Morgan would guarantee the "trading obligations" of Bear and its subsidiaries, providing "management oversight" for its business. The Fed would provide "special financing" as part of the deal, the release added, to the tune of $30 billion in funding for Bear's "less liquid assets."

The release contained the requisite complimentary quotes from Dimon, who stated that his company would "stand behind Bear Stearns," and from Schwartz, who called the deal "the best outcome" for "all constituencies" after what had been "an incredibly difficult time" for the company. But the detail that stopped most readers cold came at the end of the second paragraph: The transaction "would have a value of approximately $2 per share."

That valued the mighty Bear Stearns, once Wall Street's fifth-biggest investment bank with a market value of $25 billion, at a paltry $236 million—less than a quarter of what its building alone was worth.

Some of the Street's hardiest veterans couldn't believe their ears. Nearby at 1585 Broadway, where they were preparing for first-quarter earnings the following week, Morgan Stanley executives like John Mack and chief financial officer Colm Kelleher wondered aloud whether the $2 was a mistake. Some Citigroup honchos, who were on an operating-committee conference call when the news broke, similarly thought the figure must be at least $20 and that someone had left the zero off. Sallie Krawcheck, head of the bank's wealth-management business, clapped her hand over the phone and signaled her husband, who had once worked at Bear and had held a number of shares. "Did you sell your stock?" she asked him in a stage whisper. He nodded. Sitting at a Knicks game in Madison Square Garden with his son, Glenn Schorr, the UBS AG securities analyst, thought the coworker who called to tell him must have been joking. He asked the man to repeat the figure as he held the cell phone closer to his ear.

In the fourth-floor equities department of 383, Pat Lewis was sitting with Jeremy Hill in his office. The two had spent what seemed like hours hitting the REFRESH command on Hill's Bloomberg terminal, waiting for news on a deal. Several hours earlier, Hill had sent a junior staffer out to the local liquor store to stock up on booze. They were drinking cheap red wine and munching on potato chips when word of the $2 deal began to get around. Hill was aghast. Lewis was resigned. He already had one foot out the door.

On the seventh floor, Jeff Mayer decided it was time to address the troops. Climbing onto a trading desk, he straightened up and announced that the deal had been done at $2 per share. He was angry about the price, he said, but "we're going to make the best of it. I know you guys have worked your hearts out, and we'll do our best to make sure that most of you get hired." With the low ceilings above the mortgage-securities area, his head was even with the overhead light fixtures, adding a strange visual quality to an already surreal experience.

A group in Friedman's office had dusted off some bottles of wine and scotch they'd been given by clients over the years and were drinking the contents from paper cups. Some of the bottles had the dates of the deals they were meant to celebrate inscribed on their labels—deals that now seemed like faint memories.

Sitting with his longtime colleagues, Friedman looked through some of the concerned e-mails he'd received from friends that weekend. Eventually, he wrote back to a poker buddy, summing up his thoughts: "We [*sic*] sitting around the office drinking through all the scotch and wine we can find," he wrote. "It's like being at a wake. 27 years, a ton of friends . . . all gone. The firm has been good to me over the years and we live pretty frugally so we're fine. Not so for the people who work for me who will be crushed."

Tim Greene, who had been in Friedman's office when the deal was announced, wandered back to his desk and began calling the members of his ten-person team to break the news. "Bear was bought by JPM," he told each. "The price is $2 per share. I'm sorry." It took an hour to get through the entire list. When he was finished, he climbed into his car, began driving home to Connecticut, and broke down in tears.

In Summit, New Jersey, David Kim got his third and final call at home from his boss. "It's over," she told him. "J.P. Morgan is buying us for two dollars a share."

Kim couldn't believe it. Hearing the news felt like that moment during an exam when the teacher said, "Pencils down," just as he was answering a question. We'd always had the reputation of handling risk very well, Kim later thought. We lived through two world wars. But we couldn't handle the credit crisis.

Reeling from the news, Upton was headed for his own office on the sixth floor when he saw a commotion there. Steve Meyer had corralled Molinaro in the treasurer's office and closed the door, which locked automatically. Upton could see the equities chief hollering at the CFO, but could hear only snatches of conversation. "How could you sell the company for two dollars?" Upton thought he heard. Meyer was standing a couple of feet from Molinaro, gesticulating wildly. Molinaro appeared to be standing his ground, quietly taking the beating.

Upton waited awkwardly until the talk died down. Eventually, the door opened and Meyer hurried out. Molinaro sank into a chair and looked at the treasurer.

"There are going to be opportunities," he told Upton. "You're a very talented guy. We've had a great run over the last couple of years. It's a shame it had to end this way."

Upton could only agree.

8:30 P.M.

Schwartz had summoned the firm's management and compensation committee for an emergency meeting in one of the twelfth-floor dining rooms. Bear employees needed to be informed of the deal, and of their obligations to return to work the following morning, despite the change of ownership. It was an important detail among what seemed like a million that had to be addressed before Monday's markets opened in New York. Schwartz needed the help of those gathered—among them Meyer, Metrick, Molinaro, and Mayer—to get it all done.

He had barely begun to brief the group when Meyer went off.

"Two dollars?" Meyer asked. "It's crazy." He gave Schwartz a cold, hard stare. "We should have sold the mortgage positions," he said, his voice rising. "I told you this would happen."

For months, Meyer and another senior stock trader, Wendy de Monchaux, had been demanding that Marano downsize his portfolio. Mortgage assets were increasingly shaky, they argued, and it was time for a dose of Ace Greenberg's long-held philosophy: Sell the losers before they're worth even less. Schwartz had understood their point, but was reluctant to sell the assets into a distressed market, where they'd be worth a pittance. Eventually, he had urged Marano to begin selling, but the size of his holdings had remained in the tens of billions.

Now Schwartz, who had tried desperately to remain calm, began losing his cool. He was sick of hearing Meyer whine.

"Steve, you don't think people worked around the clock to figure this out?" he yelled. "What do you want us to do? We are where we are."

Meyer continued to rant. The firm should have sold its toxic assets three months ago, he shouted back. Schwartz should have listened back then, when it could still have made a difference.

"You know," said Schwartz, "we just don't need this. We've got to move on. Why are you wasting our time?"

Meyers looked offended. "I've got better things to do," he said.

"Good," said Schwartz. "Leave. Now. I only want people here who are going to help get something done."

The two stared at each other for what seemed like a long time, with neither saying anything. Meyer didn't move, and Schwartz continued glaring at him. Finally, Jeff Mayer, the head of fixed income, broke the silence. "Come on," he said softly. "Let's settle down."

Marano, still fuming about the deal price, walked in at the tail end of the confrontation. For months he and Meyer had disagreed about the direction his business was taking—and not just about the amount Marano held in mortgages. Bear had always been a place where traders could disagree and still remain friends. But there was no point to the argument now. The mortgage head claimed a seat at the table and listened quietly while Schwartz walked through the hours and days to come.

The $2 deal wasn't all that had emerged that evening. At 7:16, the Bear executives learned an astonishing fact: The Federal Reserve, after months of lobbying, would allow investment banks to borrow directly from it, rather than restricting its lending facility, known as the "discount window," just to commercial banks. The Fed's action reversed decades of policy—and came about two hours too late to help Bear.

Schwartz was on an industry conference call with Dimon, Geithner, Paulson, and most of Wall Street's most senior executives when the Fed's move was finally discussed. Hearing the details of the new lending facility, which would open for business on Monday, his stomach sank. Schwartz felt devastated for Bear, seeing what the company could have avoided. But he also knew that without a lender of last resort—a role the Fed would now play for his rivals on the Street—firms like Lehman Brothers might not last the week.

A little while later, Parr caught up with Schwartz in the hallway. Parr was blinking back a tear, and Schwartz's eyes were watery, too.

"Alan," said Parr softly, "you should feel very good about what you've accomplished in getting this done. You've done a remarkable job in working this through."

Schwartz shook his head, trying to collect himself.

"I feel terrible," he finally said.

EPILOGUE

Bear Stearns, as it turned out, was only the first in a long string of financial firms to suffer mortal harm. Faced with the same toxic combination of income losses and dwindling market confidence, a slew of other brokerages and lenders failed or came close to failing in the months that followed. By September 2008, just six months after Bear's sale to J.P. Morgan, the investment banking industry had effectively ceased to exist.

Yet even to some of the market's most sophisticated players, the expansion of the crisis wasn't immediately obvious. Bear's deal with J.P. Morgan, which was finalized at the end of May, came during a period of relative calm. The Federal Reserve's opening of the discount window to investment banks had provided a measure of renewed faith. Moreover, Bear's mixed reputation as a firm of gunslingers with little aptitude for hedging or risk management made its failure easy to dismiss by bigger, seemingly stronger parties.

Blue chip stocks actually rose that spring, with the Dow Jones Industrial Average topping 13,000 for a brief period in May. Rival chief executives were sounding notes of cautious optimism. "We're probably in the third or fourth quarter" of a four-quarter game, Goldman chief Lloyd Blankfein told investors in early April. During that month John Mack, Morgan Stanley's CEO, made similar remarks.

All, however, was not well. Lehman Brothers, the century-and-a-half-old investment firm that had been Bear's closest competitor in size and scope, in June reported its first loss since going public in 1994. At the same time Merrill Lynch, the nation's largest brokerage firm, was buckling under the weight of $55 billion in toxic mortgage assets. Both companies were raising capital, but investor faith in their futures was waning nonetheless.

Danger was brewing on other fronts. In early July, IndyMac Federal Bank, the large Southern California savings-and-loan company and the country's seventh-largest mortgage issuer, failed after sustaining massive losses from its portfolio of largely risky home loans. Soon after, Fannie Mae and Freddie Mac, the government-sponsored corporations that owned or guaranteed half the country's residential mortgages, came under severe pressure. Fears that the companies lacked adequate capital had driven their share prices down to their lowest levels since the mid-1990s.

Regulators quickly stepped in. In late July, Congress approved a bill to give the Treasury and the Fed increased oversight of Fannie and Freddie, including the ability to provide them with an unknown amount of financial assistance and to nationalize the entities if their positions became sufficiently tenuous. Despite howls of protest from some lawmakers, in early September, Hank Paulson did just that, placing the corporations in government "conservatorship." In what the *Wall Street Journal* dubbed the government's "most dramatic market intervention in years," the Treasury invested $1 billion in each company, removed their CEOs, and vowed to extend up to $200 billion in additional assistance as Fannie and Freddie continued to absorb losses from failing U.S. home loans.

Markets reacted well to the news, which was viewed as a vote of confidence in the U.S. housing sector and an indication that mortgage rates might fall in the months to come. But their reprieve was short-lived, as the crisis quickly returned to the investment-banking sector.

Both Lehman and Merrill had by then reached a breaking point. Lehman had managed its way through the beginning of the residential-mortgage crisis, but its large commercial-mortgage portfolio had led to major losses. The firm had warned of up to $4 billion in write-downs for the third quarter of the year, and was faltering in its efforts to raise new capital. Existing lenders were demanding additional billions in collateral, and credit-rating agencies had threatened a downgrade that would make getting credit even tougher.

Merrill had off-loaded some of the dangerous mortgage assets that threatened to ruin confidence, but its balance sheet was still far from clean. Just as they had with Bear, clients were pulling some of their money out, and Merrill's stock price was sagging badly.

The government, however, had taken a defiant stance. Paulson had refused another investment-banking bailout, and in three days of emergency meetings at the New York Federal Reserve Bank, Tim Geithner urged the remaining Wall Street firms to work bailout plans on their own. They didn't entirely succeed. Late on Sunday, September 14, Merrill was sold on the fly to Bank of America Corp., the large depositor based in Charlotte, North Carolina. In the wee hours of the following morning, Lehman filed for bankruptcy.

Regulators viewed Lehman's failure, at least in part, as a cautionary tale for investment banks and the markets—a guard, after months of government intervention to salvage faltering companies, against moral hazard. The popular opinion was that Lehman CEO Dick Fuld and his board had had months to raise more capital or do a deal to sell their firm, and seeing the company go belly-up, turning twenty-five thousand employees onto the street, was the result of their incompetent stewardship.

But the bankruptcy proved disastrous for both Lehman and its industry survivors. On September 16, the government announced an $85 billion guarantee to backstop the flailing insurer American International Group, whose cash position had been badly compromised. Once again a company had been nationalized after proving unable to run itself. Financial stocks were punished brutally in the days that followed, with particular duress on Morgan Stanley—now one of the only two investment banks left on Wall Street. In addition to a sagging stock price, Morgan, like Bear, was now facing a huge exodus by hedge fund clients who feared their money might not be safe in the firm's coffers anymore.

That weekend, the CEOs of Morgan and Goldman took matters into their own hands. Investors in the market seemed more comfortable with banks than investment banks, preferring the former category's lower appetite for risk taking and oversight by the Federal Reserve rather than the SEC. So, hoping to avoid the stomach-churning denouements their peers had endured, on September 21 they announced plans to become bank-holding companies rather than investment banks—giving up their longtime structures for good.

The destruction of wealth and jobs—indeed, an entire way of life on Wall Street—has been stunning. Since Bear's senior executives gathered for their first of many emergency meetings in Molinaro's conference room that Thursday night in March, the Dow has plunged by nearly a third—erasing trillions of dollars of investor profits. At this writing, in February 2009, unemployment in the United States reached nearly 8 percent, reflecting the loss of 3.6 million jobs since late 2007, when the current economic recession officially began. The trend is expected to continue at least until the end of 2009, with some economists expecting another 2 million jobs to fall away.

The loss of money and jobs has had a domino effect on the economy. Consumer spending has plummeted, as evidenced by the leanest holiday shopping season in years, prompting a wave of bankruptcies in the retail sector. In Detroit, the big three automakers, once the backbone of American manufacturing, are struggling for survival. Housing prices, whose initial declines spurred the troubles at Bear and other lenders and banks, have fallen precipitously. As the wave of defaults and delinquencies on home loans persists, many U.S. neighborhoods are now dotted with boarded-up homes and diminished public services, leading to new waves of crime.

Many jobless citizens face stacks of unpaid bills and a lack of access to health care. The paucity of benefits has driven some to extreme lengths. One pregnant cookie-factory worker in Ohio asked her midwife to induce labor, hoping her baby could arrive before her health insurance was cut off after her company's bankruptcy filing. But the baby didn't arrive in time, and the Cesarean section she ended up needing rendered her twenty thousand dollars in medical debt.

States and communities are struggling to meet their residents' needs. Some, like St. Louis, Missouri, plan deep cuts in local transportation services, moves that could force hundreds of bus commuters out of their jobs. California, faced with a $40 billion shortfall in the state's budget, has ordered 200,000 state workers to stay home two days a month in order to save on payroll costs. In New York in early January, the state's online unemployment insurance system, besieged by thousands of inquiries, shut down twice in two days.

In the brief amount of time since Bear's collapse, conventional wisdom already holds that Bear hung itself by carrying around an unwieldy $30 billion portfolio of risky mortgages—a state that practically invited lenders to back away and traders to short its stock. But those holdings, in fact, were of higher quality than most people realize, and ultimately told only part of the story of Bear's demise.

Bear failed because the credit crisis of 2008 killed every firm with a large mortgage business, too little diversification to offset the losses from bad loans, and the inability to be proactive. Those factors ruined Lehman Brothers, and, directly or indirectly, almost sank Fannie, Freddie, AIG, and Merrill Lynch—until the government, private industry, or both stanched the bleeding.

But among the investment banks that once dominated the U.S. economy, Bear, the fifth largest, was also uniquely vulnerable. The simple spirit that made Ace Greenberg the company's most celebrated figure—that of cutting losses early, saving money on paper clips and envelopes, and guarding religiously against outsized risk—

had long since been replaced by a more cavalier outlook. Its chief proponent was Jimmy Cayne. Handsomely paid and disinterested in details, Cayne embraced Greenberg's philosophy in the most narrow-minded sense. He watched expenses, funding his own helicopter service to and from the office and railing against pay and title inflation in the company's more junior echelons. He stuck to what the company knew, fighting the expansion into new services and territories that some of his deputies were advocating. In so doing, he kept Bear's business mix in the backwoods and let risk management deteriorate. Cayne himself lacked the patience to micromanage Bear's hedges, so he left that work to an overburdened Warren Spector, an aging Greenberg, and a handful of technical models.

Nowhere was this shortfall more evident than in the failure of the two High-Grade hedge funds in 2007.

The reversal in subprime loans in early 2007 affected Ralph Cioffi, their manager, badly, and his funds' performance went directly south.

Investor confidence was lost, and creditors were leery. Several, including J.P. Morgan, had thrown Cioffi's funds into default—only to be dismissed by Warren Spector, who told J.P. Morgan executives at the time that he didn't understand what they were dealing with. Cioffi's pleas for clemency—delivered at a pair of meetings with creditors in June—made him for a time a laughingstock. Bear was the firm that refused to bail out Long-Term, whose CEO wouldn't leave his office for a meeting and who would fight a rival firm over a turkey sandwich, much less an interest rate on a loan. Now one of Bear's money managers had proven himself incompetent. The lenders felt it was absurd that Cioffi expected them to give him a break on collateral demands or a grace period on margin calls.

So the curtain lowered on Cioffi's funds, and soon, in short order, on Spector, Bear's profitability, and Cayne himself. In August and September 2008, Ace Greenberg and Steve Meyer began arguing with Tom Marano over the size of his mortgage portfolio. They didn't like his holdings, or his hedge—a huge short bet on financial firms like Wells Fargo and Wachovia that he referred to as "the chaos trade." Marano's antagonists eventually forced him to unwind that short, which was on its way to making $1 billion. But his mortgage holdings remained largely intact.

Alan Schwartz's elevation to CEO in January 2008 could have been the panacea Bear needed. An investment banker with three decades of experience, Schwartz made his living advising companies—sometimes troubled ones—on how to climb out of holes and grow business. Deals and capital raising were his forte.

But Schwartz, like many Bear employees, was in denial about his company's travails. To him, the fourth-quarter loss had been a painful blip, and he had faith that the first quarter's earnings would turn Bear's reputation back around. Schwartz was focused on management restructuring and beefing up its efforts to mitigate risk— both noble objectives, but more appropriate for a company with better prospects.

But when capital-raising opportunities came around in January and February, Schwartz essentially dismissed them. Several investments had already fallen through, and he had grown wary of the opportunities that were out there. Plus, Schwartz didn't want to distract people from the good news that was coming. His departure for Palm Beach on March 6 may now seem naïve, but it was unclear, even then, that Bear was failing.

In the aftermath of Bear's sale to J.P. Morgan, many middle and senior managers were infuriated by what they perceived as Schwartz's blindness to Bear's glaring problems. The Nomura and Sumitomo investments were there for the taking, they believed, and Bear's CEO arrogantly blew it. But the hard truth is that a few billion dollars at that point would not have been enough. The only better alternative would have been an outright sale to some larger suitor, but few people realized that at the time.

Schwartz testified at a Senate Banking Committee hearing on April 3. Alongside Dimon and Geithner, he relayed his version of the events surrounding Bear's toppling. There he acknowledged he "had always had a concern" that investment banks' lack of access to the Fed discount window could be a problem. "I just never frankly understood or dreamed that it could happen as rapidly as it did," he said.

"I just simply have not been able to come up with anything," Schwartz added, "even with the benefit of hindsight, which would have made a difference."

Some investors would argue it was laughable to put an investment banker in charge of a sales-and-trading firm in the first place. Given his limited purview, Schwartz could not, perhaps, have predicted that Bear's bad reputation had again returned to haunt it. During the week of March 10, as shares skidded amid a haze of negative rumors, its ardent refusal to bail out Long-Term Capital Management ten years before came up more than once. One trader joked to me that Bear should just sell itself to J.P. Morgan for $250 million and be done with it—a shockingly low suggestion of a sale price at the time.

Citing such anecdotal evidence, some people assert that Bear was driven out of business not just by lenders and clients with legitimate worries but also by a cabal of predatory traders who had bet big on the company's fall. Conspiracy theories hold that a group of hedge funds known as the "breakfast club" formulated a plan to load up on credit default swaps, or insurance protection policies that would pay out if Bear was toppled, early in March. Legend has it that those parties then shorted Bear's stock while simultaneously opting out of their own longstanding transactions with Bear, spreading chatter about the company's travails. Though this theory has been oft discussed on Wall Street and among securities cops, no hard evidence has emerged that it actually happened.

Regulators may never know the truth. But one thing is clear:

Once confidence in a company falls away on such a grand scale, it can never recover. Bear started that week with more than $18 billion in capital, its largest cash position ever. Three days later, negative headlines, a stock drop, lender reticence, and big withdrawals from client accounts had cut those capital levels in half. Eight hours later, it was nearly dead.

Bear's $2 sale to J.P. Morgan wasn't the end of the story. In the days that followed the hurried Sunday-night deal, shareholders made clear their resistance to such a low price. Early the following morning, a weary Schwartz was confronted in Bear's gym by an irate trader. "How could this happen to fourteen thousand employees?" the trader, Alan Mintz, demanded. "Look in my eyes, and tell me how this happened!" Three days later, at a town-hall meeting with SMDs that J.P. Morgan had convened as a show of faith, Jamie Dimon found himself in a similar position when an outraged Bear broker compared the bank's purchase of his company to a "rape."

Realizing its sweetheart deal might be on the rocks, J.P. Morgan began negotiating for a larger stake in Bear that would essentially guarantee the acquisition. But Schwartz, who wanted a higher price for the company, was unbending.

That Easter weekend the stakes ratcheted up. J.P. Morgan threatened to stop guaranteeing Bear's liabilities if a new and more attractive deal was not reached by Monday. Bear briefly considered suing the bank to force it to honor its original deal terms. Regulators were alerted to the problem, and Bear's board again convened for a weekend of tense discussions, this time away from 383 Madison at Rodge Cohen's downtown offices. They were now facing Chapter 7 bankruptcy—total liquidation—rather than Chapter 11, which allows for reorganization. Bear's business had further deteriorated during the week following the $2 deal, making the firm even weaker than it had been before.

Early on Monday, March 24, J.P. Morgan presented its final offer:

$10 per share—or a price of $1.2 billion for the company—in exchange for nearly 40 percent of Bear's outstanding stock, a stake that edged the deal closer to certainty. To make the deal more palatable for the government, the bank also agreed to absorb the first $1 billion of any losses on the Bear mortgage portfolio that the Fed had guaranteed, leaving the central bank with $29 billion in exposure. Bear's board, mollified somewhat by the higher price, accepted the new terms.

Directors may have acted in the firm's best interests, but as shareholders, many remained deeply unhappy. The day after the new deal was approved, Jimmy and Patricia Cayne sold their entire Bear holdings—some 5.7 million shares—for a profit of $61.3 million. The next week, Paul Novelly, one of Bear's independent directors, followed suit. Many other Bear insiders, whose holdings accounted for about 30 percent of the public float before the deal with J.P. Morgan, were left to marvel at the erosion of wealth in their portfolios. Two months later, at the May 29 shareholder meeting at which J.P. Morgan's purchase was finalized, Cayne took responsibility. "I personally apologize," he told those gathered, fiddling with the microphone as he spoke. "Words can't describe the sadness that I feel." The deal was approved by 84 percent of Bear's investors.

The weeks that followed were brutal for Bear's fourteen thousand employees, who waited anxiously to discover who would be laid off, who would be hired, and who would stay on as "transitional" employees to help with the integration. Understanding how agonizing it was, J.P. Morgan took pains to ease the process. Dimon asked a number of key clients, including General Electric, to consider hiring from Bear's pool of talent, and the bank set up a large outplacement service to help identify new job opportunities.

Ultimately, some sixty-five hundred Bear workers were hired by J.P. Morgan. Despite some dark humor over the resultant culture clash—one running joke among Bear alums is that JPM, where corporate planning is far more structured than it was at Bear, stands for "just people meeting"—many of those hired as a result of the deal say they have been bowled over by their new colleagues' friendliness and cordiality. Some also admit that J.P. Morgan's severance payouts, which were based on a person's tenure at Bear, were more generous than Bear's might have been.

Still, the process hasn't been without its tragic moments, chief among them a death in Bear's ranks. Late in May, just days before the deal's finalization, Barry Fox, a manager in Bear's research department, took his own life after learning he would not be kept on board. He had only eleven shares of Bear stock at the time, according to his companion, but the idea of living with no job and a combination of bad health conditions made it difficult for him to see the future.

Bear's former leaders have scattered since the destruction of their company. All but one declined to stay on board at J.P. Morgan for any significant length of time.

Schwartz remained through the finalization of the deal, saying he would decide whether to take Dimon up on his offer of a senior post if J.P. Morgan treated Bear employees well. In what appeared to be an initial vote of confidence, Schwartz continued working out of 383 Madison—now J.P. Morgan's building—and advised his longtime clients on the bank's behalf for several more months. But by Labor Day, he had parted ways with J.P. Morgan and took a gig at Rothschild, the small British investment bank, along with longtime partner Richie Metrick.

In the year since Bear's failure, Schwartz has kept a strenuously low profile, declining media interviews and saying little about his trial. His one regret, according to associates, is that the discount window wasn't opened sooner. If it had been, he believes, Bear might well have survived.

Schwartz brought clients like Microsoft, Disney, and Cablevision to Rothschild, where his friend Christopher Lawrence is vice chairman. Schwartz remains rueful about what came to pass, say associates, and uncertain about his own future, despite job offers from buyout firms and other banks. After his thirty-two years at Bear that ended so tragically, he isn't sure he's ready to open shop at another large institution. He continues to be a trustee of Duke University, his alma mater, and was recently named chairman of the Robin Hood Foundation, a charity dedicated to relieving poverty in New York City.

Sam Molinaro also has yet to put down roots. He, too, stayed with J.P. Morgan for some months to help with Bear's integration while eyeing the landscape for other opportunities. At fifty years old and with plenty of energy, he told friends he didn't want his job as chief financial officer of a failed investment bank to be his epitaph.

Late in 2008, he signed on with the successful hedge fund Paulson & Co., Bear's former prime-brokerage client and sometime nemesis, as a consultant. He has yet to find the right full-time job.

After a short-lived role at the investment adviser Primerica, in January 2009 Bob Upton landed as treasurer of the brokerage firm Cantor Fitzgerald. Comparing Cantor to an old-school Bear Stearns, Upton has told associates that, after a difficult period of uncertainty in his career, he is fired up and ready to get to work at his new employer.

Bear's integration with J.P. Morgan did not sit well with Tom Marano, who found the bank's directives about trading to be confusing and its attitude toward risk taking unproductive. After a contentious period in March and April, he left Bear for a new job as chairman and CEO of Residential Capital, the residential-mortgage unit of GMAC LLC, the lender owned largely by General Motors.

As part of his new job, for which he commutes from Madison, New Jersey, to ResCap's offices in the suburbs of Philadelphia, Marano has dealt with more of the same problems that beset Bear. ResCap has lost money, adding to GMAC's already considerable struggles, and has laid off thousands of workers.

Paul Friedman now works at Mariner Investment Group, a hedge fund based in Westchester County, New York. It is run by former

Bear executives Lee Sachs and Bill Michaelcheck and is affectionately known by firm alumni as "Bear North."* Friedman has told friends that his five-minute driving commute from Scarsdale is far too short, and that he misses his evening nap on the train ride home from Manhattan. Never a bull, he continues to worry about the deteriorating state of the financial markets.

Jimmy Cayne remains in retirement. He spends time golfing and relaxing at his second home near the Jersey Shore, and recently took an extended holiday at a Boca Raton resort. Cayne continues to play on the international bridge circuit, and visited Boston in November 2008 for the North American tournament. He plans to follow that, say friends, with a trip to Australia in February 2009.

Ace Greenberg now works at J.P. Morgan, where his title is vice chairman emeritus. He is penning a memoir about his experience at Bear. At age eighty-one, he comes to the office every day and still works with his longtime clients.

*Early in 2009, Sachs took a leave from Mariner to go to Washington, where he is expected to take on a senior role at the U.S. Treasury, working for his old friend Tim Geithner.

NOTES

Thursday

14 *reducing their balance levels:* Kate Kelly, "The Fall of Bear Stearns: Fear, Rumors Touched off Fatal Run on Bear Stearns," *Wall Street Journal,* May 28, 2008.

17 *Thursday morning brought another big blow:* Kate Kelly and Serena Ng, "In Dealing with Bear Stearns, Wall St. Plays Guardedly," *Wall Street Journal,* March 13, 2008

18 *"clients are leaving us":* Kate Kelly, "The Fall of Bear Stearns."

Thursday Evening

25 *Bear refused to participate:* Roger Lowenstein, *When Genius Failed* (Random House, 2000).

26 *scantily clad models:* Michael Siconolfi, "Talented Outcasts: Bear Stearns Prospers Hiring Daring Traders That Rival Firms Shun," *Wall Street Journal,* November 11, 1993.

26 *liked to put out his cigars:* The Wall Street Journal, *Who's Who and What's What on Wall Street* (Ballantine Books, 1998).

26 *small stock-trading house:* "A History of Bear Stearns," graphic, *New York Times,* March 17, 2008.

27 *distressed quasi-public investments:* Charles Kaiser, "Salim L. Lewis, Wall St. Pioneer in Stock Block Trading, Dies at 69," *New York Times,* May 1, 1978.

36 *an embarrassing tussle:* Kate Kelly and Serena Ng, "The Sure Bet Turns Bad Funds Howl as Bear Stearns Buys Mortgages," *Wall Street Journal,* June 7, 2007.

38 *pleaded for the chance:* Matthew Goldstein and David Henry, "Bear Bets Wrong; Two Bear Stearns Hedge Funds Soared," *BusinessWeek,* October 22, 2007.

39 *emergency $3.2 billion loan:* Kate Kelly and Susanne Craig, "Losing Hand: How Bear Stearns Mess Cost Executive His Job," *Wall Street Journal,* August 6, 2007.

39 *reassure the public:* Kate Kelly and Randall Smith, "Remodeling Job: Market Swoons as Bear Stearns Bolsters Finances—Brokerage Raises

Cash, Cuts Short-Term Debt; Spector Expected to Exit," *Wall Street Journal,* August 4, 2007.

40 *Bear had already taken another step:* Kate Kelly and Susanne Craig, "Losing Hand: How Bear Stearns Mess Cost Executive His Job."

48 *He was at a restaurant in Anguilla:* Bryan Burrough, "Bringing Down Bear Stearns," *Vanity Fair,* August 1, 2008.

Friday

62 *$46 trillion market:* International Swaps and Derivatives Association, Inc., Web-published market survey, 1987–present (2008).

65 *Hoping to stabilize their teetering economy:* Aurel Schubert, *The Credit-Anstalt Crisis of 1931* (Cambridge University Press, 1991).

72 *Corzine hid in his town car:* Craig Horowitz, "The Deal He Made," *New York,* July 10, 1985.

74 *it was heading toward $100 billion:* Julie Creswell and Ben White, "Wall Street, R.I.P.: The End of an Era," *New York Times,* September 28, 2008.

79 *"People realized that Bear Stearns":* Kate Gibson, "Market Snapshot: U.S. Stocks Briefly Collapse on Bear Stearns," *Dow Jones Business News,* March 14, 2008.

Later Friday

85 *Cayne had introduced . . . fast friends:* Kate Kelly, "Losing Hand: How Bear Stearns Mess Cost Executive His Job," *Wall Street Journal,* August 6, 2007.

86 *spoke out on behalf of Senator John Kerry:* "Bids & Offers," *Wall Street Journal,* August 6, 2004.

104 *Bear's Dallas office in 1976:* Landon Thomas, "Bear Stearns Heir Apparent Tries to Restore Some Faith," *New York Times,* August 7, 2007.

108 *Cayne had been hospitalized:* William D. Cohan, "The Trials of Jimmy Cayne," *Fortune,* August 4, 2008.

108 *On November 1:* Kate Kelly, "Bear CEO's Handling of Crisis Raises Issues," *Wall Street Journal,* November 1, 2007.

111 *PIMCO, had admonished:* Kate Kelly, "The Fall of Bear Stearns: Lost Opportunities Haunt Final Days of Bear Stearns," *Wall Street Journal,* May 27, 2008.

Saturday

134 *site had already pointed out:* Kate Kelly, "Where in the World Is Jimmy Cayne? Playing Bridge," *Deal Journal,* March 14, 2008.

136 *when Cayne was still a stockbroker:* Cohan, "The Rise and Fall of Jimmy Cayne," *Fortune,* August 18, 2008.

136 *His market-risk gatherings . . . "you're out, O-U-T":* Michael Siconolfi, "Talented Outcasts: Bear Stearns Prospers Hiring Daring Traders That Rival Firms Shun," *Wall Street Journal,* November 11, 1993.

137 *He excoriated employees who left their desks:* Alan C. Greenberg, *Memos from the Chairman* (New York: Workman Publishing, 1996).

137 *in another partner memo:* Ibid.

138 *Rubin was fired:* Siconolfi, "Talented Outcasts," *Wall Street Journal,* November 11, 1993.

139 *stripped of his job:* Charles Gasparino, "Bear Stearns Ex-Official Stiffly Fined," *Wall Street Journal,* April 21, 2000.

140 *to settle the charges:* Randall Smith and Tom Lauricella, "Moving the Market: Bear Stearns to Pay $250 Million Fine," *Wall Street Journal,* March 17, 2006.

Later Saturday

143 *"I hear and I absorb":* Cohan, "The Rise and Fall," *Fortune,* August 18, 2008.

144 *New York City's financial crisis . . . lacked "balls":* Ibid.

145 *part of a longstanding bet:* Landon Thomas, Jr., "Quarrel Erupts Between Bear's Elder Statesmen," *New York Times,* May 7, 2008.

145 *"completely on my side":* Cohan, "The Rise and Fall," *Fortune,* August 18, 2008.

146 *In 2003, Bear for the first time:* U.S. Securities and Exchange Commission, Bear Stearns Co., Form 10-K, February 27, 2004.

146 *richest chief executive:* Susanne Craig, "The Biggest Fish on Wall Street? Probably Not Who You Think," *Wall Street Journal,* May 9, 2006.

147 *famously told associates:* Kelly, "Bear CEO's Handling of Crisis," *Wall Street Journal,* November 1, 2007.

148 *when Lewis began loading up on Bear shares:* Roddy Boyd, "Lewis Raises Cayne—Helps Bridge Gap," *New York Post,* September 12, 2007.

148 *forced him to buy:* Cassell Bryan-Low and Kate Kelly, "Credit Crunch: Bear Succumbs," *Wall Street Journal,* March 17, 2008.

153 *accompanied by friends:* Kelly, "Bear CEO's Handling of Crisis," *Wall Street Journal,* November 1, 2007.

157 *Cayne gave an interview:* Landon Thomas, Jr., "Salvaging a Prudent Name," *New York Times,* June 29, 2007.

158 *Spector had personally authorized:* Cohan, "The Rise and Fall," *Fortune,* August 18, 2008.

160 *"important to be seen":* Kate Kelly and Dana Cimilluca, "Can New CEO Repair Bear?," *Wall Street Journal*, January 9, 2008.

162 *Countrywide claimed to account for some 16 percent:* U.S. Securities and Exchange Commission, Countrywide Financial Corp., Form 10-K, March 1, 2007.

Sunday

189 *In a column written:* Gretchen Morgenson, "Rescue Me: A Fed Bailout Crosses a Line," *New York Times*, March 16, 2008.

190–191 *In graduate school . . . "part of the group":* Shawn Tully, "In This Corner! The Contender," *Fortune*, March 29, 2006.

191 *Dimon was exposed to the financial world . . . Weill's personal assistant:* Monica Langley, *Tearing Down the Walls* (New York: Simon & Schuster, 2003).

193 *began taking boxing lessons . . . penchant for financial services:* Langley, *Tearing Down the Walls.*

193 *"my one big shot":* Shawn Tully, "The Jamie Dimon Show," *Fortune*, July 22, 2002.

194 *"want them to bleed":* Ibid.

195 *"Forget the visionary stuff":* Robin Sidel, "Deals & Dealmakers: For Dimon, Another Shot," *Wall Street Journal*, January 19, 2006.

196 *"dumbest thing," "baby finger,"* and *"Roman Empire":* Tully, "In This Corner," *Fortune*, March 29, 2006.

196 *"showed up at my door":* Tully, "The Jamie Dimon Show," *Fortune*, July 22, 2002.

196 *"He loves misbehaving":* Tully, "In This Corner."

196 *One infamous confrontation:* Langley, *Tearing Down the Walls.*

Epilogue

217 *$55 billion in toxic mortgage assets:* Susanne Craig et al. "The Weekend That Wall Street Died—Ties That Long United Strongest Firms Unraveled as Lehman Sank Toward Failure," *Wall Street Journal*, December 29, 2008.

218 *"most dramatic market intervention in years":* James R. Hagerty et al., "U.S. Siezes Mortgage Giants—Government Ousts CEOs of Fannie, Freddie; Promises Up to $200 Billion in Capital," *Wall Street Journal*, September 8, 2008.

221 *twenty thousand dollars in medical debt:* Ianthe Jeanne Dugan, "For Workers, Medical Bills Add to Pain as Firms Fail," *Wall Street Journal*, December 6, 2008.

221 *bus commuters out of their jobs:* Michael Cooper, "Rider Paradox: Surge in Mass, Drop in Transit," *New York Times,* February 3, 2009.

222 *didn't understand what they were dealing with:* Bryan Burrough, "Bringing Down Bear Stearns," *Vanity Fair,* August 1, 2008.

225 *"how this happened":* Kate Kelly, "The Fall of Bear Stearns: Lost Opportunities Haunt Final Days of Bear Stearns," *Wall Street Journal,* May 27, 2008.

225 *an outraged Bear broker:* Kate Kelly, "The Fall of Bear Stearns: Bear Stearns Neared Collapse Twice in Frenzied Last Days," *Wall Street Journal,* May 29, 2008.

225–6 *That Easter weekend . . . accepted the new terms:* Ibid.

226 *"I personally apologize":* Kate Kelly et al., "The Fall of Bear Stearns: Bear's Final Moment," *Wall Street Journal,* May 30, 2008.

227 *"Barry Fox, a manager":* Kate Kelly, "Crisis on Wall Street: His Job at Bear Gone, Mr. Fox Chose Suicide," *Wall Street Journal,* November 6, 2008.

BIBLIOGRAPHY

I am grateful to have had access to the following works, which aided my research and writing:

Bill Bamber and Andrew Spencer. *Bear Trap: The Fall of Bear Stearns and the Panic of 2008.* New York: Brick Tower Press, 2008.

Bryan Burrough and John Helyar. *Barbarians at the Gate: The Fall of RJR Nabisco.* New York: HarperCollins, 1990.

Alan C. Greenberg. *Memos from the Chairman.* New York: Workman Publishing, 1996.

Alan Greenspan. *The Age of Turbulence: Adventures in a New World.* New York: Penguin, 2007.

David M. Kennedy. *Freedom from Fear: The American People in Depression and War, 1929–1945.* New York: Oxford University Press, 2005.

Paul Krugman. *The Return of Depression Economics and the Crisis of 2008.* New York: W. W. Norton & Co., 2009.

Monica Langley. *Tearing Down the Walls.* New York: Simon & Schuster, 2003.

Roger Lowenstein. *When Genius Failed: The Rise and Fall of Long-Term Capital Management.* New York: Random House, 2000.

INDEX